> Fit für die **Oberstufe**

Englisch

Schroedel
westermann

› Fit für die **Oberstufe**

Englisch

Autorinnen:
Christiane Huber arbeitet als Englisch- und Sportlehrerin an einem bayerischen Gymnasium. Im Jahr 1999/2000 unterrichtete sie am Presbyterian Ladies' College in Melbourne/Australien.
Cornelia Klameth unterrichtete an einem bayerischen Gymnasium Englisch, Spanisch, Sport und Deutsch als Zweitsprache. Seit Februar 2015 arbeitet sie an der deutschen Auslandsschule Santa Ursula in Lima/Peru. Sie studierte ein Semester an der Universität in Norwich/England.

Mit Beiträgen von Jens Bolhöfer, Cordula Dopichei, Hyacinth Moodalie-Hünnemeyer und Anke Strauß.

westermann GRUPPE

Druck[5] / Jahr 2020

Redaktion: imprint, Zusmarshausen
Kontakt: lernhilfen@westermanngruppe.de
Layout und Umschlaggestaltung: Janssen Kahlert Design und Kommunikation GmbH, Hannover
Umschlagfoto: plainpicture, Hamburg
Illustrationen: Hans-Jürgen Feldhaus, Münster
Satz: imprint, Zusmarshausen
Druck und Bindung: Westermann Druck GmbH, Braunschweig

ISBN 978-3-507-**23012**-5

Vorwort

Liebe Schülerin, lieber Schüler,

Sie wollen fit werden für die Oberstufe?
Dieses Buch hilft Ihnen, Ihre Fähigkeiten im Fach Englisch richtig einzuordnen und das zu trainieren, was Sie noch nicht sicher genug beherrschen.

Wie arbeiten Sie mit diesem Buch?

1. Beginnen Sie mit dem Einstiegstest. Bearbeiten Sie jeweils einen Teilbereich (A bis E). Gehen Sie dabei die Aufgaben zügig an.

2. Kontrollieren Sie Ihre Ergebnisse mithilfe der Lösungen im Anhang und notieren Sie Ihre Ergebnisse im Lerntagebuch (Download unter www.schroedel.de/oberstufe).

3. Das Lerntagebuch gibt Ihnen eine Übersicht darüber, welche Themen Ihnen noch Schwierigkeiten bereiten und welche Kapitel Sie daher als Erstes bearbeiten sollten. Am Ende jedes Kapitels können Sie im Zwischentest Ihren Lernfortschritt überprüfen.

4. Nachdem Sie alle Kapitel durchgearbeitet haben, in denen Sie noch Schwierigkeiten hatten, sind Sie fit für den Abschlusstest.

Die Aufgaben in diesem Buch haben zwei Schwierigkeitsstufen, damit Sie passend zu Ihrem Leistungsniveau üben können. Besonders anspruchsvolle Aufgaben sind mit einem ★ gekennzeichnet.

Wenn Sie im Buch nicht genügend Platz zur Bearbeitung der Aufgaben finden, nehmen Sie bitte ein Heft zur Hand.

Viel Erfolg beim Üben mit ***Fit für die Oberstufe***!
Christiane Huber und Cornelia Klameth

Inhaltsverzeichnis

Lerntagebuch

Mit dem Lerntagebuch Wissenslücken effizient schließen!

Im Eingangstest schon Wissenslücken entdeckt?
Dann planen Sie Ihren weiteren Lernfortschritt mit dem Lerntagebuch.
Dieses finden Sie unter:

www.schroedel.de/oberstufe

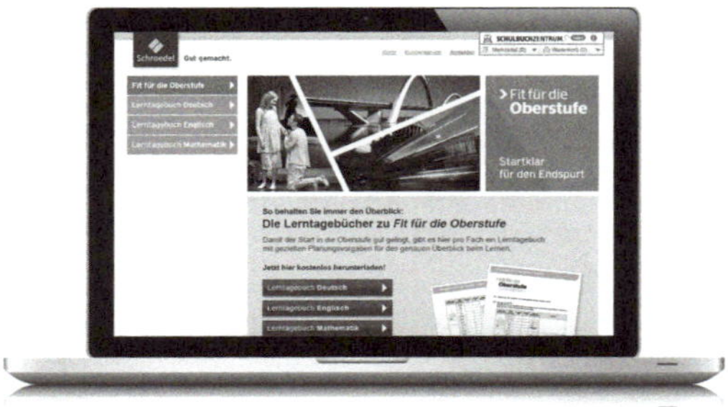

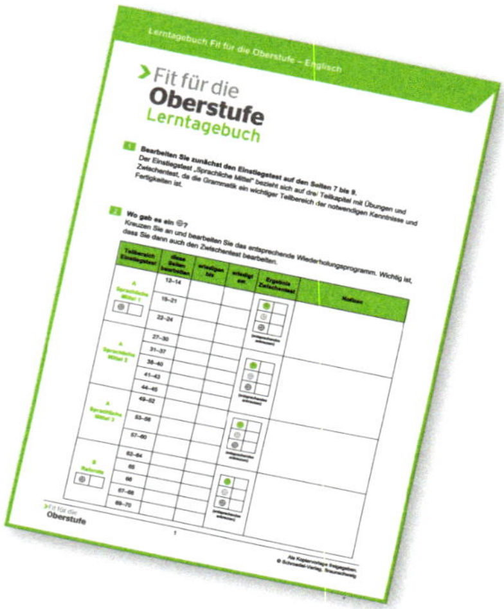

Das Lerntagebuch gibt Ihnen einen genauen Überblick darüber, welche Themen noch Schwierigkeiten bereiten und welche Kapitel daher als Erstes bearbeitet werden sollten.

So behalten Sie beim Lernen immer den Überblick und der erfolgreiche Start in die Oberstufe ist gesichert.

Einstiegstest

Bad Memories

In her memoir 'Please stop laughing at me', Jodee Blanco describes how as a teenager she was constantly bullied by her classmates. Today, Blanco is a successful business woman and teaches publishing at New York University and the University of Chicago.
Read the extract below.

When I reached out to take his hand, he gripped my wrist and started **twisting** it until my knees began to **buckle**. Then, Kat, Dara, Jackie, and several other students came at me from behind. They grabbed my hands and feet and dragged me across the parking lot behind the main campus, chanting "We're going to kill you." They started kicking me and spitting on me. They ripped open my bookbag and threw the contents all over the ground.
Oddly, I wasn't frightened. Being killed held the promise of relief.
Lying on the pavement, curled up in a ball, listening to them laugh at me, all I could think of was how I was going to explain what happened to me when I arrived home. My jacket and pants were ripped and **filthy**. My hair was full of gravel and spit. My arms were scratched and bruised.
I remained there in the **fetal position**, rocking back and forth until the bell rang and I heard my **tormentors** leave. I sat up and opened my eyes. I gathered my books and papers and slowly stood up. I was in terrible pain. Not knowing what else to do, I went to the nurses' office.
"I was running to class and fell," I **fibbed**. "I ruined my sweater, so I put my gym shirt back on." The nurse, a **persnickety** woman, stared at me, disbelief written all across her face.
"Could you help me clean up?" I asked, **wincing**. "These cuts really hurt."
"Jodee, you're not telling the truth," she observed, sternly.
"Please, I can't be a **tattletale** again. Let me handle this my own way," I begged.
"All right, but if I see you in this state again, I'm contacting your parents," she said.
"Fair enough."
Though she did as much as she could for me, the signs of the attack were still **visible**. "Are you all right?" Ms. Gorge inquired as I eased myself carefully into my desk.
Every eye in the room was on me. If I said anything to Ms. Gorge, I'd be digging my own grave.
"I tripped and fell."
"Do you want to go home?" she asked. "No, I'm okay." [...]
I **dreaded** my parents finding out that I was a social **failure** again, so every afternoon when I got back from school, I carefully hid any evidence of abuse. I applied makeup to my arms and legs so my mom couldn't see the bruises where I'd been punched or kicked.
I **soaked** the bloodstains and mud off my clothes in the tub before she got home. If I had to cry, I turned the stereo on so no one could hear me. When anyone asked how school was going, I said that everything was terrific and that I'd never been happier.
Mr. Warren and Ms. Gorge had to know something was wrong, but they never said or did anything. One afternoon, Steve and Dara followed me to the school bus.
"What's wrong?" Dara hissed. "Are you afraid?"

"Why should you be afraid of us?" Steve **cooed ominously**. "We're your friends." I thought I might **throw up**. "Come on, you guys. Just leave me alone." They both burst into laughter. Now, I didn't care what happened to me. I was **seething with rage**.

"Go to hell, you bastard," I cried. Then Steve hit me in the chest so hard that it knocked the wind clean out of me. Struggling to catch my breath, I fell to the ground and **sobbed**.

Mr. Warren saw me as he was getting into his car, and came over.

"What happened?" he asked.

"Steve hit me. I want you give him a detention," I demanded. "I want him to get in trouble."

"Jodee, I could give him a detention. What he did was wrong. But don't you think it would be better if you and Steve worked out your problem between the two of you without school intervention? If I give him a detention, you're only going to be labeled a tattletale. In the real world, we must learn to fight our own battles," Mr. Warren said patronizingly.

Now I felt more alone than ever. "I guess you're right."

Bad Memories, from: Please stop laughing at me, by Jodee Blanco, Adams Pub 2003

twist – turn
buckle – become weak and bend
filthy – dirty
fetal position – position of the unborn baby
tormentor – s.o. who makes s.o. suffer severe pain
fib – not telling the truth
persnickety (American) – caring too much for details
wince – show pain
tattletale (American) – s.o. who likes to tell bad things about other people
visible – able to be seen
dread – be afraid of doing sth.
failure – here: looser
soak – put sth. into a liquid and leave it there for a long time
coo – say sth. nicely
ominous – making you think that s.th. bad will happen
throw up – be sick
seethe with rage – become very angry
sob – cry

A Sprachliche Mittel

**1 Questions: Imagine Jodee's parents finally find out about their daughter being a victim of bullying. They want to know everything about it.
Can you ask six of her parents' questions?**

1. ....
....

2. ....
....

3. ....
....

4. ....
....

5. ....
....

6. ....

....

6

2 Reported Speech: Rewrite the paragraph using reported speech.
"Jodee, I could give him a detention. What he did was wrong. But don't you think it would be better if you and Steve worked out your problem between the two of you without school intervention? If I give him a detention, you're only going to be labelled a tattletale. In the real world, we must learn to fight our own battles," Mr Warren said patronizingly.
Start like this:

Mr Warren answered ....

....

....

....

....

....

....

....

....

7

★ **3 Passive: The following sentences are all taken from the extract. Can you rewrite them using the passive instead of the active where possible? Be careful, some phrases can't be changed.**

lines	sentences in the active
3–5	They grabbed my hands and feet and dragged me across the parking lot behind the main campus.
4	They (were) kicking me.
5	They ripped open my bookbag and threw the contents all over the ground.
28–29	... so every afternoon when I got back from school, I carefully hid any evidence of abuse.
32–33	When anyone asked how school was going, I said that everything was terrific and that I'd never been happier.

5

Gesamtpunktzahl Aufgaben 1 bis 3 18

Kontrollieren Sie Ihre Ergebnisse mithilfe der Lösungen (S. 110) und addieren Sie die erreichten Punkte.
Teilbereich A: ☐ 18 bis 14 Punkte: ☺ ☐ 13 bis 9 Punkte: 😐 ☐ 8 bis 0 Punkte: ☹

B Referate

4 **You have to give a presentation about "bullying at school". Think of an interesting introduction using the text "Bad Memories".**

3

5 **Auf welche formalen Kriterien müssen Sie bei einer Computerpräsentation achten?**

7

10 **Gesamtpunktzahl Aufgaben 4 und 5**

C Lesen

6 **Read the statements and find evidence from the text that they are true. Underline the relevant parts in the text.**

a) Her tormentors avoided having witnesses for their terrible behaviour.
b) The attack was not the first one.
c) Jodee could not speak about the attack in front of her class.
4 d) Mr. Warren does not really help her. He wants to avoid a conflict.

7 **Answer the questions using your own words as far as possible.**

a) What did the tormentors do with Jodee?
6 b) What did Jodee do to hide any evidence of abuse?
c) Why did she not inform her parents?

★ **8** **Interpretation: Mr Warren observed the incident at the bus station. His reaction made Jodee feel more alone than ever. What did she really think of the situation and her teacher's attitude towards bullying?**
6

16 **Gesamtpunktzahl Aufgaben 6 bis 8**

Kontrollieren Sie Ihre Ergebnisse mithilfe der Lösungen (S. 110/111) und addieren Sie die erreichten Punkte.

Teilbereich B:	☐ 10 bis 8 Punkte:	☐ 7 bis 5 Punkte:	☐ 4 bis 0 Punkte:
Teilbereich C:	☐ 16 bis 13 Punkte:	☐ 12 bis 8 Punkte:	☐ 7 bis 0 Punkte:

D Schreiben

9 **Write a summary of the extract from Jodee Blanco's memoir "Please stop laughing at me" in about 100 – 150 words.** 6

10 **After Jodee has been bullied yet again, she asks her teacher for help. He answers, "Jodee, I could give him a detention. What he did was wrong. But don't you think it would be better if you and Steve worked out your problem between the two of you without school intervention? If I give him a detention, you're only going to be labeled a tattletale. In the real world, we must learn to fight our own battles."**
Do you think what the teacher tells her is right?
Comment on his answer.
(300 – 400 words) 12

★ 11 **Creative writing (100 – 200 words)**
What might have happened before the other kids started bullying Jodee? 8

Gesamtpunktzahl Aufgaben 9 bis 11 26

E Mediation/Sprachmittlung

★ 12 **An American exchange student at your school has read the following article in a magazine and doesn't understand it. Explain what it is about.**

Der Feind in meiner Schule

An Deutschlands Schulen werden täglich Tausende Jungen und Mädchen von Klassenkameraden geschnitten, gehänselt, geschlagen sowie persönlich oder über Mobiltelefone und Internet-Portale beschimpft, gedemütigt, bedroht. Mobbing ist an Schulen „ein ernst zu nehmendes Problem", lautet das Ergebnis einer Studie. 43 Prozent gaben an, von ihren Mitschülern gehänselt zu werden. Jeder fünfte berichtete von Schlägen. Manchmal, beim sogenannten Happy Slapping, filmen Täter Prügelszenen mit dem Handy und verbreiten die Videos per MMS oder Internet.

Aus: http://www.focus.de/schule/schule/psychologie/psychoterror/tid-14378/deutschland-der-feind-in-meiner-schule_aid_397574.html (gekürzt)

Gesamtpunktzahl Aufgabe 12 10

Kontrollieren Sie Ihre Ergebnisse mithilfe der Lösungen (S. 111/112) und addieren Sie die erreichten Punkte.

Teilbereich D:	☐ 26 bis 21 Punkte: 🙂	☐ 20 bis 13 Punkte: 😐	☐ 12 bis 0 Punkte: 🙁
Teilbereich E:	☐ 10 bis 8 Punkte: 🙂	☐ 7 bis 5 Punkte: 😐	☐ 4 bis 0 Punkte: 🙁

Sprachliche Mittel – 1

Vorschau

→ Present tenses
→ Past tenses
→ Future tenses

Present tenses

REGEL: Mit dem ***simple present*** (einfache Gegenwart) spricht man über **regelmäßig stattfindende Dinge und Handlungen**, über **Tatsachen**, **Gewohnheiten** oder **dauerhafte Zustände**. Typische **Signalwörter** für diese Zeitform sind: ***always, usually, often, sometimes, never, every day/month..., regularly, on Tuesdays ...***
Man bildet das ***simple present*** durch den einfachen Infinitiv des Verbs. In der dritten Person Singular wird ***-s*** oder ***-es*** an das Verb angehängt; Verben, die auf Konsonant + ***-y*** enden, verändern sich in der dritten Person Singular in ***-ies***:

I take → it takes ***we go → she goes*** ***they try → he tries***

Um **Fragen** oder **negative Aussagen** zu bilden, verwendet man das Hilfsverb ***do*** 3. Pers. sing.: ***does***) mit dem Infinitiv.

Do you like school?/Does she always walk the dog?
I don't like school very much./She doesn't walk the dog every day.

Mit dem ***present progressive*** (Verlaufsform) spricht man über Handlungen, die zum Zeitpunkt des Sprechens passieren oder die über einen längeren Zeitraum in der Gegenwart (nicht unbedingt zum Zeitpunkt des Sprechens) stattfinden. Die Verwendung dieser Zeitform ist aber nur bei Verben möglich, die eine Tätigkeit ***(go, sing, make)*** oder einen Vorgang ***(become, get)*** ausdrücken.
Typische **Signalwörter** sind ***(right) now, at the moment, just.***
Man bildet das ***present progressive***, indem man eine Form von ***be*** verwendet und ***-ing*** an das Verb anhängt. Ein stummes ***e*** vor ***-ing*** entfällt. Ein Konsonant wird verdoppelt, wenn der vorangehende Vokal kurz ist.

go → she **is** ***going*** ***take → I*** **am** ***taking*** ***get → we*** **are** ***getting***

Einige Verben erscheinen in der Regel **nicht in der Verlaufsform**:

- Verben der Wahrnehmung ***(feel, smell, sound, look, taste)***;
- Verben des Gefühls ***(love, hate, want, wish, like, refuse)***;
- Verben, die geistige Prozesse ausdrücken ***(think, believe, realize, mean, agree, know, forget, remember)***;
- Verben, die Besitzverhältnisse ausdrücken ***(own, belong, possess)***;
- modale Hilfsverben ***(can, must, may, shall, will)***;
- sowie ***be*** (im Sinne von Existenz) und ***have*** (im Sinne von Besitz).

1 Put in the correct form of the verb – simple present or present progressive.

Original sound

The club (1) .... (fill) up fast on Friday nights. It is no different this Friday. The crowd (2) .... (move) in rhythm to the pulsating beat as the DJ (3) .... (manipulate) his **turntables** and (4) .... (create) an irresistible groove propelled by a driving beat. As the lights flash, two women (5) .... (appear) on stage. While one woman (6) .... (sing) a haunting melody, the other (7) .... (call) out to the audience and then begins to rap about her life. The words (8) .... (speak) about drugs, gangs and violence, being lost and being found and surviving life off the reservation.
The three people on stage (9) .... (form) a group called *Original* that (10) .... (gain) **acclaim** in the city for their compelling blend of hip-hop and native rhythms. John Burnwood, the DJ and spokesperson for the group (11) .... (be) an eighteen-year-old Aboriginal living in Winnipeg, Canada. He (12) .... (currently share) a small, **dilapidated** house in the north end of the city with his twin sisters Jessie and Wendy who are also members of *Original*. John Cree's heritage (13) .... (play) a vital role in his daily life and he (14) .... (attribute) the strength to cope with the urban poverty that typifies his neighbourhood to the spiritual practices of his people. "It (15) .... (be) easy to become lost here," states John, "I still (16) .... (go) to school, but I know a lot of guys who (17) .... (be) in jail. In this neighbourhood, if you are Indian, you have a higher chance of going to prison than of graduating from High School."
John and his sisters started *Original* two years ago. "
We (18) .... (find) our inspiration in the stories of our people

both past and present and because we all (19) .... (love) hip hop, it was a natural progression to mix it with the beats we heard at the Pow-wows. And rap is the perfect music for us because it combines rhythm and story-telling."

"It was from going to Pow-wows with my Dad that I found my talent for music and participating in the **Sweat lodges** gave me a sense of my importance and my future. A lot of kids (20) .... (not know) the stories of our people, they (21) .... (not have) respect for themselves and so they (22) .... (fall) into crime because it (23) .... (give) them a sense of importance." When asked about the audiences' reactions to their music, John hesitates before answering. "Sometimes I (24) .... (think) that just seeing the three of us on stage shocks people. People (25) .... (not can) always figure us out, but once I start mixing, people start dancing and when people dance, they open their minds. So when they (26) .... (hear) Jessie and Wendy sing, they are already open to an experience and that is what we try to give them."

---

turntable – flat round part of a record player
dilapidated – old and in a bad condition
acclaim – public praise for s.o. or sth.
Sweat lodge – indian sauna, here: dance hall, disco

2 Are the underlined verbs in the right tense? Correct where necessary.

a) Water <u>freezes</u> at 0 degrees Celsius. ....

b) He <u>reads</u> a book about music right now. ....

c) I am usually <u>riding</u> my bike to school. ....

d) In the morning, he <u>is exercising</u> for an hour before breakfast. ....

e) She <u>is learning</u> how to speak Chinese at present. ....

f) I <u>am living</u> with my uncle right now. ....

g) With the advancements in manufacturing, the price of DVD players <u>falls</u>. ....

h) He <u>touches</u> his forehead in amazement. ....

i) They <u>don't telling</u> us anything anymore. ....

j) They <u>are moving</u> to Moose Jaw, Saskatchewan, right now. ....

k) Every time I <u>am calling</u> him, he does his homework. ....

l) The protestors are <u>demonstrating</u> against the increased tuition fees now. ....

Past tenses

REGEL: Es gibt **verschiedene Zeitformen** im Englischen, um Vergangenheit auszudrücken.
Man benutzt das ***simple past***, um über etwas zu berichten, das in der Vergangenheit stattgefunden hat und abgeschlossen ist. Außerdem werden Handlungsfolgen (z. B. in Erzählungen) im ***simple past*** wiedergegeben. Die typischen Signalwörter verweisen auf eine spezifische Zeit in der Vergangenheit, z. B. ***yesterday, last week ..., a year ago, in 1988.*** Man bildet die Form, indem man bei regelmäßigen Verben ***-ed*** oder ***-d*** an den Infinitiv anhängt. Unregelmäßige Verben haben eigene ***past tense***-Formen, die man wie Vokabeln lernen muss.

phone → phoned ***take → took*** ***love → loved;***
cut → cut ***cry → cried*** ***go → went***

Das ***past progressive*** betont die Dauer einer Handlung während eines bestimmten Zeitraums in der Vergangenheit. Die Zeit wird mit ***was/were* + Verb in der *-ing*-Form** gebildet.

Yesterday Jack was preparing a presentation in the afternoon.

Fanden in der Vergangenheit mehrere Vorgänge gleichzeitig statt, wird bei allen Vorgängen das ***past progressive*** verwendet.

While Jack was looking for information on the internet, his sister was listening to music.

Ist eine Handlung schon im Gange, während eine andere Handlung einsetzt, steht die „alte" Handlung im ***past progressive*** und die „neue" im ***simple past***.

The family was having dinner when the doorbell rang.
(alt) (neu)

Mit dem ***present perfect simple*** gibt man Handlungen wieder, die in der Vergangenheit begonnen haben und bis in die Gegenwart reichen. Vorsicht: Im Deutschen steht in diesem Fall Präsens! Man bildet die Zeit durch eine **Form des Hilfsverbs *have* und des Partizip Perfekts** (3. Verbform).

I have known Jack for five years now. – Ich kenne Jack nun schon seit fünf Jahren.

Außerdem werden Handlungen beschrieben, die gerade beendet sind.
Im britischen Englisch wird dabei häufig das Signalwort ***just*** verwendet.

Mark has just phoned his friend.

Das ***present perfect simple*** beschreibt auch Handlungen oder Ereignisse, die schon beendet sind, aber Auswirkungen auf die Gegenwart haben.

He has finished his homework and is ready to play now.

Außerdem wird es verwendet, wenn etwas schon einmal, häufig oder noch nie passiert ist.

Have you ever seen a whale ? – Yes, I've seen lots.

Typische Signalwörter für eine Zeitspanne in der Vergangenheit sind ***for*** und ***since***.
Ohne eine bestimmte Zeitangabe sind typische Signalwörter ***never, ever, always, already, still, so far, until now, (not) yet, recently***.

REGEL: Das ***present perfect progressive*** betont die Dauer einer Handlung und drückt aus, dass etwas in der Vergangenheit begonnen hat, aktuell andauert und vielleicht auch noch in der Zukunft weitergehen wird. Typische Signalwörter sind hier ebenfalls oft ***for*** und ***since***. Die Zeitform wird gebildet durch
eine Form von *have* + Partizip Perfekt + Verb + *-ing*

> ***Oh dear, what have you been doing all morning?***
> ***She has been surfing the Internet for ages.***

Um innerhalb der Vergangenheit Vorzeitigkeit auszudrücken, benutzt man das ***past perfect***. Es zeigt an, dass eine Handlung in der Vergangenheit vor einer anderen in der Vergangenheit liegenden abgeschlossenen Handlung (***simple past***) stattgefunden hat. Die Zeitform wird gebildet durch ***had* + Partizip Perfekt** (dritte Verbform).

> ***He had already done his homework when I got home.***

Bei dynamischen Verben kann auch hier die ***progressive form*** verwendet werden (***past perfect progressive***), wenn die Dauer bzw. der Ablauf einer Handlung betont werden soll.

> ***They had been talking for thirty minutes before Mary interrupted them.***

3 Simple past or present perfect? Put the verbs in brackets into the correct form. Be careful: sometimes the passive form is needed.

Model United Nations conference

Two days ago six Year 10 students from Millingdale Middle/Grammar school (1) .... (take part in) the Model United Nations Conference which, (2) .... (hold) in New York City. "The experience (3) .... (be) fantastic!" said James the star of the show, who (4) .... (just admit) that before flying out of London Heathrow airport, he (5) .... (feel) so nervous, that he (6) .... (consider) catching the next train home to the safety of his room. Fortunately for the Indian Delegation (represented by Millingdale), he (7) .... (overcome) his anxiety.
James' debating skills (8) .... (earn) him a lot of praise so far. This (9) .... (confirm) in New York where he (10) .... (win) the Best Speaker Award at the Conference. Public speaking (11) .... (teach) James **to think** quickly and logically **on his feet**. It (12) .... (give) him an opportunity to learn

about political, social and global issues which affect us all.

Moreover, he (13) .... (gain) greater self confidence.

Since James (14) .... (begin) debating in year 8, first as a member of the debating society and then in year 9 for the MUN group, his overall grades (15) .... (improve).

"I (16) .... (strengthen) my reading, writing, listening and speaking abilities. Until now, preparing for debates (17) .... (be) similar to revising for exams but far more exciting: Yes, I would highly recommend debating to my fellow students. It's absolutely awesome! I can't believe that I (18) .... (visit) the UN building and (19) .... (have) a chance to meet with international UN representatives, both the professionals as well as their 'younger' counterparts," (20) .... (report) James, beaming with pride.

think on one's feet – react/decide quickly

★ **4 Present perfect simple and present perfect progressive.**

a) Paragraphs **(A)** and **(B)**: Underline all the verb forms in the present perfect in red and in the present perfect progressive in green. Give reasons for the choice of tense.

Modern technology in Malaysia

(A) Information and communications technology (ICT) has revolutionized the world we live in. As a result, all individuals, including those less privileged and in developing countries, should enjoy access to the resources and digital opportunities that ICT allows.

(B) Samal Ali, a 16 year old Malaysian, living in Kuala Lumpur, has been surfing the net and building web sites since he was 14. Despite his humble origins, Samal has found a way to broaden his interest in computer technology. His parents could not afford to buy him a computer so he decided to approach an insurance company near his school and offer his services. In exchange for doing odd jobs, he has gained access to one of the in-house computers. The initial half an hour per day has since increased to several hours and what started out as "playing around" has now developed into a lucrative part-time job for Samal.

b) Paragraphs **(C)** and **(D)**: put the verbs in brackets in the present perfect simple or present perfect progressive. Sometimes you have to use the passive form.

(C) He .... (1) (carry out) data entry tasks,

.... (2) **(troubleshoot)**

when there have been technical difficulties. He .... (3) (also/build) web sites for the company as well as many of their clients for the past two years. Although the company .... (4) (not always comply) with the Malaysian employment laws, there is often a convenient **loophole** somewhere. Samal affirms he .... (5) (not be exploit) in any way. On the contrary, he feels he .... (6) (be reward) for his efforts. Once he .... (7) (complete) his work duties, he may do research for school projects and finish homework tasks using the computer.

(D) At times, Mr and Mrs Ali worry that Samal .... (8) (neglect) his studies for several months. Yet, the extra income .... (9) (prove) a welcome contribution for the family. For some time now Samal's parents .... (10) **(flathunt)**. Their present living quarters, a 35 square meter flat, can barely accommodate the needs of a family of four. Samal .... (11) (scan) the on-line **real estate** advertisements for possibilities. Normally, a family of their social and economic status would not have access to these ads. With a little luck, the Ali family may succeed in improving their standard of living and benefiting from ICT.

---

troubleshoot – solve problems
loophole – sth. left out of a law that people can use to avoid obeying it
flathunt – to look for a place to live
real estate – business of buying and selling land, houses and flats

Simple past and past progressive

5 Put the verbs in brackets in the correct form of the simple past or past progressive.

a) While Sam .... (play) the piano, his teacher suddenly .... (sneeze).

b) I .... (travel) to Munich the day Princess Diana .... (die).

c) Many students .... (study) for the Maths test when the fire alarm .... (go off).

TIPP

Signalwort für das ***past progressive*** ist **while**, für das ***simple past*** hingegen **when**.

d) Just as the Prime Minister .... (deliver) his speech, a bomb .... (explode) at a nearby subway station.

e) When the One Direction concert .... (begin), Jane and her friends .... (still sit) on the train to London.

f) Cristiano Ronaldo .... (raise) his arms in victory when the referee .... (declare) a foul.

g) When I .... (be) young, my parents .... (always nag) me about my homework and now I do the same with my children.

h) Since the traffic .... (move) so slowly, Mr Stearn .... (can) not get to the examination centre on time.

i) "I .... (only make) a suggestion!" .... (shout) John's mother.

j) Students .... (line up) for their enrolment forms when the university librarian .... (make) an announcement to evacuate the building immediately.

Simple past, past perfect and past perfect progressive

6 **Read the following text and check the tenses (simple past/past perfect). There are ten mistakes in it. Underline them and write down the correct tense.**

The Canterville Ghost

[...] The second appearance of the ghost was on Sunday night. Shortly after the family went to bed they had heard a fearful crash in the hall. A suit of armour fell on the floor and in a chair sat the Canterville ghost and rubbed his knees, which seemed to hurt. When the twins had started shooting peas at him with their pea-shooters, the ghost stood up with an angry growl and passed through them like a mist. He also had blown out the candle, leaving them all in total darkness. On top of the stairs the ghost turned around and, in order to frighten the Otis boys, laughed his most horrible laugh. Just then, a door had opened and Mrs Otis came out of her bedroom. "I am afraid you are

not well," she said, "I have therefore brought you this bottle of medicine." The ghost looked at her furiously, and then he had disappeared.
When he reached his room, he had been completely exhausted. This American family was extremely annoying. But what annoyed him most was, that he was not able to wear the suit of armour. The weight of it made him fall and hurt his knees. [...]

http://www.ego4u.com/en/read-on/literature/canterville-ghost?part3

Mixed tenses

7 Write the interview between reporter Anne Peters and the Latin pop star idol, Shakira. Be careful to use the right tenses. Signal words will help.

Example: Reporter – Question: how long / sing
Q: ***How long have you been singing***
Shakira – Answer: since / child
A: ***I've been singing since I was a child.***

Q: when/start/write/own songs

....

A: 8 years old

....

Q: Your father is Lebanese. Ever/visit/Lebanon

....

A: yes/Arabic sounds/influence my music/ever since.

....

Q: true/Columbian singer Juanes/big fan of yours

....

A: yes/be a wonderful man/always very encouraging

....

Q: I hear/you/take/a particular interest/politics

....

A: yes/as I be born in Colombia/always/be important to me.
When/live there/be always involved in politics.

....

....

Q: you able/keep Latin American creativity/with new English language songs on the "Laundry Service Album"

A: well/write in English/be a real challenge. Spend/long time/beforehand/ read poetry/and that/certainly/help

Q: can/expect/hear/more English songs from you

A: definitely/not mean I not also continue/write songs in Spanish.

Q: one final question before/time run out/when you launch next album.

A: be much sooner/than you think.

Q: thank you for time/we look forward to new release.

A: Find an appropriate answer and a polite goodbye.

Future tenses

REGEL: Im Englischen gibt es **verschiedene Möglichkeiten**, über Zukünftiges zu sprechen. Neben der Verwendung der ***future tenses*** können auch **Zeitformen der Gegenwart mit Signalwörtern** ***(tomorrow, next year, later today, this evening, tonight, some day)*** auf Handlungen in der Zukunft verweisen.

Das ***will-future*** benutzt man, um über Ereignisse in der Zukunft zu sprechen, die **wahrscheinlich sind** und **vermutlich passieren** werden. Außerdem drückt es **spontane Entschlüsse** aus.
Es wird gebildet durch ***will* + *Infinitiv***.

> ***When I am 18, I will get my driver's licence. I'll help you after supper.***
> ***Shall we dance? (Do you want to dance?)*** → für spontane Vorschläge

Man benutzt das ***going-to-future***, um **feste Vorhaben in der Zukunft** auszudrücken. Dabei ist eine Zeitangabe nicht unbedingt nötig.
Man bildet die Zeitform, indem man eine **Form von *be* + *going to* + *Infinitiv*** verwendet.

> ***She is going to talk to your maths teacher tomorrow.***
> ***I'm going to read that book (this summer).***

Alternativ zum *going-to-future* kann das ***present progressive*** in Aussagen verwendet werden, die **einen festen Plan** ausdrücken. Dabei wird eine Zeitangabe der Zukunft gemacht.

> ***He is moving to Canada this summer. I am getting married tomorrow.***

Das ***simple present*** wird im Zusammenhang mit Zukünftigem verwendet, wenn es um **Zeitpläne** (TV/Kino), **Programme** und **festgelegte Termine** geht. Auch hierbei wird eine Zeitangabe gemacht.

> ***The game is on television at 4:00 this afternoon.***

Das ***future progressive*** verwendet man, um über Ereignisse zu sprechen, **die zu einem zukünftigen Zeitpunkt gerade ablaufen.** Es bezieht sich auch oft auf eine Zeitspanne in der Zukunft, während der eine Begebenheit oder Handlung stattfindet, aber nicht abgeschlossen wird.
Es wird gebildet durch ***will be* + Verb + *-ing***.

> ***In a year from now, she'll be going to school.***
> ***Please don't call us between 5:00 and 6:00, we will be watching the news.***

Das ***future perfect*** zeigt an, dass **Ereignisse und Handlungen vor einem bestimmten Zeitpunkt in der Zukunft beendet sein** werden. Es wird gebildet durch ***will have* + Partizip Perfekt** (dritte Verbform):

> ***I will have done it by Sunday.***
> ***Do you think the problem will have been solved by then?***

8 Fill in the correct verb forms in the right future tense.

A year in "Down Under"

Each year, hundreds of teens from across Germany participate in International exchange programs. Popular choices for students include Canada, the United States, the United Kingdom and Ireland. The International Exchange Programme provides teens with a year long opportunity to live in an English-speaking environment and to experience first-hand English culture. Like many of her peers, Allison Schmidt is excited about participating in the program. However, unlike any of her fellow students, Allison's exchange experience (1) .... (be) one long trip down under. In just a few short weeks, Allison Schmidt (2) .... (go) to Australia for an International Student Exchange program where she (3) .... (live) in Wollongong, New South Wales, just outside of Sydney. "I've always wanted to go to Australia and now I (4) .... (actually/live) there and will go to school too!" exclaims Allison. "I spoke with my host family and they have already told me that I (5) .... (see) kangaroos and koalas every day. And they (6) .... (have) a 'Barbie' on the beach for me when I get there. Of course, we (7) .... (go) to Sydney, but what I really hope to do is to go scuba diving at the Great Barrier Reef in Queensland." But it won't be all barbies and 'roos' for Allison, "It (8) .... (be) very exciting, but it' (9) .... (be) hard too" declares Allison. "I (10) .... (be) in an Australian School and I don't know if anyone (11) .... (speak) German. My English is OK, but having to speak it all the time (12) .... (be) really tough. My sister told me that after a few weeks, I (13) .... (talk) like the Crocodile Hunter, but I don't know if I (14) .... (even be able to) understand the teachers. If that happens, I don't know what I (15) .... (do)." Although participants are often excited to explore their host countries, the International Exchange Program focuses mainly on educational achievements. Allison's year in Wollongong (16) .... (feature) an accelerated academic program that includes courses in calculus, English Literature, History and foreign languages. However, the heavy course load does not daunt Allison. "This (17) .... (be) the greatest experience I've ever had," states Allison. "Even though I (18) .... (miss) my family and friends, I think it (19) .... (be) fantastic." "Maybe my sister is right," muses Allison. "In a year, I (20) .... (speak) more English than I could have imagined possible. I (21) .... (be surrounded) by Australians, I (22) .... (experience) a totally different culture and I (23) .... (learn) to speak English, just like they do in Down Under!"

9 **Answer the questions using the correct future tense.**

a) Where exactly is Allison going?

....

....

b) What kind of animals will she see?

....

c) Who will she miss when she is in Australia?

....

d) What does she think will be difficult about the experience?

....

....

e) What courses will she be taking?

....

f) How many students are going to Australia?

....

Zwischentest

Girls and guitars

Stars like Avril Lavigne have made guitars popular with girls, writes Chloe Anthony

The guitar has always been an essential part of any rock or pop group, but the most famous guitar players have always been men. This is changing as more and more young women are playing the guitar.

There have also been famous female guitar players such as Suzi Quatro or the Bangles, but recently the music scene has seen the great success of "girl bands". At the moment, probably the most famous female guitarist is Avril Lavigne, who has inspired many young women to start learning the guitar.

Music experts say there is a general revival of the guitar today. After the heyday of the electric guitar in the sixties, the instrument went out of fashion as techno became the sound of the day. Ten years ago £30 million was spent on guitars in the UK. Last year people in the UK spent £105 million on guitars.

Five years ago in the US, Tish Ciravolo, a bass guitar player, set up the first company to produce guitars made for girls. Daisy Rock guitars are lighter with narrower necks. They come in colours like Peppermint Pink and Awesome Blue and models called Butterfly-Heartbreaker, Stardust and Rock Candy.

Tish says, "What I wanted to do was not only design a guitar for a girl to play, but to change the consciousness – make the sight of a girl playing the guitar as natural as that of a girl playing the flute. And, apart from just designing guitars that girls could play, I believed a guitar should be fun – I wanted them to be girlie – I wanted girls aged eight to 11 to say, 'Wow – I want to play!'"

So you want to play guitar in a band ... here are some tips on how to go about it. First you need a decent guitar. Second you have to practise. The best thing to do is to find yourself a teacher. If you can't, or don't have the money to pay for lessons, then you can use a book or just learn to play your favourite songs. Third, you should find a band. Ask friends, create a network, practise in the garage. Lastly, be confident, have an open mind and have fun!

Aus: Read on, November Issue 2005, page 5 – Carl Ed. Schünemann Verlag, Bremen. www.sprachzeitungen.de

1 **What tenses are used in these sentences and why?**

sentence	tense	why
Music experts say there is a general revival of the guitar today.		
This is changing as more and more young women are playing the guitar.		
... but recently the music scene has seen the great success of "girl bands".		
Last year people in the UK spent £105 million on guitars.		

8

2 **Translate the sentences into English using suitable tenses.**

a) Mein Freund sagt, dass wir eine musikalische Familie sind.

....

b) Meine Mutter singt wirklich gut und spielt Flöte.

....

c) Mein Vater begann Geige zu spielen, als er fünf Jahre alt war, sodass er das sehr gut kann.

....

....

d) Ich spiele seit zwei Jahren Gitarre.

....

e) Zurzeit nehme ich Klavierunterricht.

....

f) Nächsten Monat wird meine 6-jährige Schwester Mitglied im Chor werden.

....

....

6

14 **Gesamtpunktzahl**

Kontrollieren Sie Ihre Ergebnisse mithilfe der Lösungen (S. 113) und addieren Sie die erreichten Punkte.

☐ 14 bis 11 Punkte: 🙂 ☐ 10 bis 7 Punkte: 😐 ☐ 6 bis 0 Punkte: 😕

Sprachliche Mittel – 2

Vorschau

- → Relative clauses
- → Reported speech
- → Passive voice
- → Conditional sentences

Relative clauses

REGEL: Relativsätze sind Nebensätze, die sich auf ein Nomen im Hauptsatz beziehen. Man unterscheidet zwischen zwei Arten:

Notwendige Relativsätze *(defining relative clauses)* enthalten wichtige Informationen, ohne die der Hauptsatz allein nicht verständlich wäre. Sie beziehen sich auf das Wort, das sie näher beschreiben und werden nicht durch Kommas vom Hauptsatz getrennt.

> ***Kevin is a boy who loves nature.***
> ***This is one of the flower pots that should be watered.***
> ***A horn is the object in a car which makes a warning noise when you press it.***

Die Relativpronome ***(relative pronouns)*** können Subjekt oder Objekt des Nebensatzes sein. Für Personen verwendet man ***who***, ***that*** und ***whose***, für Sachen ***which***, ***that*** und ***whose***.

Relativpronomen können auch weggelassen werden, wenn sie das Objekt eines notwendigen Relativsatzes sind.
Solche Satzkonstruktionen nennt man ***contact clause***.

> ***The girl who/that I had seen was black. → The girl I had seen was black.***
> ***The book that you gave me was interesting. → The book you gave me ...***

Nicht notwendige Relativsätze *(non-defining relative clauses)* werden fast nur im formellen Englisch verwendet. Sie enthalten Informationen, die nicht unbedingt zum Verständnis des Hauptsatzes erforderlich sind, und werden durch Kommas vom Hauptsatz getrennt.

> ***J. K. Rowling, who is the author of Harry Potter, is one of the richest women in the UK.***
> ***My town, which was founded in 1260, is very picturesque.***

Für Personen verwendet man ***who*** oder ***whom***, für Sachen ***which***, jedoch niemals ***that***.

1 Combine the two sentences using a relative pronoun without changing their meaning. Leave the pronouns out where possible to form a contact clause. Make any other necessary changes.

a) My sister and I went to see the new Star Wars film. It was one of the best films she had seen this year.

....

....

b) Susan would really like to go to the Miley Cyrus concert. It will be in Munich.

....

....

c) The school books belonged to Milton. They were scattered on the floor.

....

....

d) In-line skating is a great way to keep fit. It helps to strengthen your muscles.

....

....

e) My mother is always complaining about the amount of time I spend on the telephone. She also carries on long phone conversations with her friends.

....

....

f) Bullying is a serious problem in many schools. We have been having class discussions on bullying.

....

....

g) Roald Dahl wrote Charlie and the Chocolate Factory. His books are appreciated by both adults and children.

....

....

h) Employment Services of Disneyland/Florida made a part time job offer to one of the students in our class. It was Paul Kramer.

....

....

i) I am reading a book. It is called Harry Potter and the Half-Blood Prince.

....

....

j) David Beckham has a cool hairstyle. I like it a lot.

....

2 Some sentences are correct and some not. Correct the mistakes where necessary and tick the sentences with no mistakes.

a) The English course what John applied for takes place in Kent, England.

....

b) The lady which came into the restaurant ordered a lunch special.

....

c) He will get the exam grade he wanted.

....

d) He told me a story what I had already heard.

....

e) They were the last group that handed in their History assignment.

....

f) Their Geography teacher to who they sent a letter lives in a very remote area.

....

g) Anorexia, which is a big problem amongst teenagers, can lead to severe physical and emotional damage.

....

h) Sandra, who her sister has been an avid supporter and member of Amnesty International, has just landed a job with their London branch.

....

....

i) Pollution in urban areas, what has become an increasingly growing concern, must be reduced.

....

j) Jenny was named School Council President, which is quite an honour.

....

★ **3 Wie sagen Sie auf Englisch, dass ...**

a) Sie die Eintrittskarten, die Sie gestern bestellt haben, heute Abend abholen können *(to pick up)*.

....

....

....

TIPP

Ein Komma benutzt man nur, wenn man mit dem ***if-clause*** beginnt.

b) ... Sie gerade eine Filmkritik über den Film, von dem Sie ihrer Freundin vor zwei Tagen erzählt haben, gelesen haben?

....

....

....

c) ... Lily James, die die Hauptrolle in „Cinderella" spielt, letzten Herbst in Berlin war?

....

....

....

d) ... Sie ein Mädchen spielt, das ohne ihre Mutter aufwächst und dessen Leben sich ändert, als sie einen gutaussehenden Fremden trifft?

....

....

....

e) ... es Leute gibt, die nur ins Kino gehen, um ihre Lieblingsschauspieler zu sehen?

....

....

....

f) ... es in vielen kleinen Städten kein Kino gibt, was schade ist?

....

....

....

Gerunds, infinitives, participles

REGEL: Das ***gerund*** ist eine **Verbform**, die dem Nomen ähnlich ist und aus dem **Infinitiv + *-ing*** gebildet wird. Dabei kann es verschiedene Funktionen im Satz einnehmen:

- Subjekt: ***Sky diving can be very dangerous***
- Objekt nach folgenden Verben: ***avoid, consider, finish, imagine, keep, (not) to mind, prefer, suggest.***
  Do you mind opening a window?
  Verben der Vorliebe oder Abneigung ***(hate, enjoy, like, love)***:
  She likes swimming.
- Nach Verb + Präposition: z.B. ***look forward to, dream of, talk about, think about, insist on, give up.***
  I'm looking forward to seeing you soon
- Nach Adjektiv + Präposition: z.B. ***afraid of, bad at, famous for, fond of, good at, interested in, keen on, proud of, tired of, used to.***
  I'm used to travelling a lot.
- Nomen + Präposition: z.B. ***chance of, danger of, difficulty in, hope of, interest in, possibility of, reason for, surprise at, way of.***
  The employees are in danger of losing their job.
- Bestimmte Ausdrücke: ***it's no use, it's worthwhile, can't help, how about, what about.***
  It's no use discussing taxes.
- Nach bestimmten Präpositionen: ***apart from, by, for, instead of, in spite of, without;***
  She got better grades by studying hard.

Der **Infinitiv mit *to*** steht nach Verben, die einen Ratschlag, eine Erlaubnis, einen Wunsch, eine Warnung oder ein Verbot ausdrücken, z. B. ***ask, advise, allow, expect, order, permit, tell, want, warn, wish***. Außerdem steht er nach Adjektiven und ihren Steigerungsformen, nach ***the first, second, ...,*** nach Fragewörtern sowie nach ***whether***.

She asked us to make our beds.
It is difficult to find a good babysitter.
He was the first to cross the Atlantic in such a small boat.
I can show you where to go.

Der **Infinitiv ohne *to*** steht nach Verben der Wahrnehmung und Verben, die eine Beobachtung ausdrücken. Darüber hinaus steht er nach fast allen modalen Hilfsverben und nach ***make s. o.*** sowie ***let***.

Steven saw five children come in and play their instrument.
He should wear his hair long, it looks better that way.
You really make me feel good!

Bei folgenden Verben gibt es **keinen Bedeutungsunterschied**, wenn man ein Gerundium oder einen Infinitiv anschließt: ***begin, start, continue, like, love, hate, intend, prefer.***

It started to rain./It started raining.

Bei diesen Verben hingegen gibt es **Bedeutungsunterschiede**: ***stop, forget, mean, regret, remember.***

stop + gerund → eine vergangene Handlung ist vorbei: ***It stopped raining.***

stop + infinitive → eine Handlung soll begonnen werden: ***I stopped to see you.***

mean + gerund → stellt eine Wirkung dar: ***If you run away, it means losing the game.***

mean + infinitive → steht für einen Plan: ***He means to become rich.***

forget, regret, remember + gerund: Bezug auf Vergangenheit

I remembered seeing her.

+ infinitive: Bezug auf Zukunft

Remember to buy some milk.

4 **You have a part-time summer job in a restaurant as a waiter or waitress. Here is a list of the rules for temporary part-time employees. Put the verbs in the correct form of the gerund or infinitive. In some cases you will have to use the infinitive without *to*.**

a) Try to arrive at work on time. If you can't avoid .... late, please call me as soon as possible. (be)

b) Remember .... your **apron** at all times and .... your hair out of your face. (wear/keep)

c) You are expected .... upon arrival and .... your order pad. (sign in/pick up)

d) Don't be afraid of .... customers .... the daily specials. (encourage/order)

e) Think about .... with customers that you have got things right. (check)

f) Let customers .... at their leisure. .... them through their meal is simply not our style. (eat/hurry)

g) If you overhear anyone .... the food, let me .... immediately. (criticize/know)

h) Never forget .... bills. Without .... them you might .... mistakes. (verify/check/make)

i) .... tips is allowed. However please remember .... them in the box so we can .... them up amongst all the employees at the end of the week. (accept/put/divide)

j) Lastly, never forget that we are interested in .... our customers so they keep .... It is therefore necessary .... friendliness and courtesy at all times. (satisfy/come back/show)

apron – sth. that you wear to protect the front of your clothes (esp. while cooking)

5 Gerund or infinitive?
In some cases the infinitive construction without *to* can be used.

A lot of teenagers enjoy .... (spend) time at raves, all night dance parties combined with choreographed laser shows. Although the majority of parents are **reluctant** .... (allow) their children .... (attend) these events, they find it hard .... (stop) them. Their arguments fall on deaf ears since peer pressure and .... (be) cool carry more weight with most teenagers. .... **(gyrate)** to the sounds of techno, trance or drum 'n' bass is sadly not the only thing that attracts so many of today's youth to this form of entertainment. At raves drug dealers are known for .... (distribute) "pocket money" club drugs such as ecstasy, LSD (lysergic acid diethylamide), GHB (gamma-hydroxybutyrate) and ketamine to young dancegoers. According to experienced ravers, club drug consumption helps .... (enhance) the stimulation or "high" they get from the event and is considered .... (not be) harmful when used responsibly. .... (take) these types of drugs, however, is far from harmless. The drugs are often mixed with other chemicals and substances, and can .... (become) highly **addictive** and .... (lead) to overdoses. In fact a high number of overdoses have occurred while clubbing. Recently strong action has been taken .... (inform) young people, parents and educators on the dangers of club drug use and .... (enforce) legal requirements for organized rave events.

Parents should .... (know) at all times what their children are doing, where they are and who they are with. By .... (curtail) rave activity there is a greater chance of .... **(curb)** drug abuse amongst teenagers. It is certainly time .... (end) this kind of teenage exploitation.

reluctant – not willing to do sth.
gyrate – to move around quickly in circles
addictive – to become dependant on; here: to cause dependancy on a harmful substance
curb – control or limit sth. that is harmful

REGEL:

Verwendung	**Partizip Präsens aktive Bedeutung!**	**Partizip Perfekt passive Bedeutung!**
Adjektiv	*This is an interesting book.*	*A broken window has to be replaced.*
Relativsätze	*Who's this girl looking out of the window (= Who's this girl who is looking ...).*	*Cars parked in this zone will be removed (= cars that are parked ... .)*
Adverbiale Nebensätze *(when, after, before, while, since, as)*	*Having finished the test, she went home (= After she had finished the test...)*	*Annoyed by the music, they left the party. (= since/as they were annoyed by ...)*
nach **Verben der Wahrnehmung**, wenn man betonen möchte, dass jemand eine Handlung beobachtet hat	*See, hear, watch, notice, smell, feel* *A few people watched the police arriving at the crime scene*	
nach **Verben der Ruhe** oder **Bewegung**, wenn man beschreiben möchte, dass zwei Dinge zeitgleich passieren	*Come, go, leave, lie, remain, stay* *The teacher left the class running downstairs.*	
nach ***keep, find, send***	*She kept making that mistake all the time.*	

6 Participles: Fill in the blanks with the present participle or past participle form of the verb.

a) .... (grin), John waved his medal in the air.

b) The hotel guests were still .... (frighten) even after the bomb threat was called off.

c) .... (hide) behind a door, the little girl felt safe from the loud party guests.

d) We saw him .... (tear) the brand new book.

e) The lawyer felt his client's .... (speak) word was as valid as a .... (write) statement.

f) .... (struggle) to reach the shore, the swimmer ploughed on with as much strength as he could muster.

g) The boy's mother came .... (scream) out of her home when she heard the news of her son's death.

h) Several victims in the recent bomb attacks were .... (stick) between the seats of the bus and failed to escape on time.

i) The last two passengers .... (wait) to board the flight appeared rather suspicious.

j) .... (drive) by jealousy, Mary slapped Vera on the cheek.

7 Combine the two sentences using a participle.

a) I saw a little girl. She was playing with her dog.

....

b) Robert had read his girlfriend's e-mail. He phoned to thank her for the good pieces of advice she had given him.

....

....

c) I heard my teacher. He was talking about an idea for a new project.

....

d) Sarah arrived home. She opened all the windows because of a terrible smell inside the rooms.

....

....

e) The politician was asked to resign because of his affair with a prostitute. He refused.

....

....

....

f) Janet saw the new CD of her favourite singer in the shop. She decided to buy it immediately.

g) Susan ran to the bus stop. She was talking to her friend on the phone to tell her she would be late.

h) Nicole Kidman is proud of her origins. She is Australian.

i) I read the book "Junk". It was written by Melvin Burgess.

★ **8 Wie kannst du mit einer Partizipkonstruktion sagen, dass ...**

a) ... du in den Ferien einen interessanten amerikanischen Jungen kennengelernt hast, der zurzeit in Berlin wohnt?

b) ... du ihn auf einer Party getroffen hast, die sein deutscher Gastbruder gegeben hat?

c) ... du die beiden über Joshs Austauschjahr in Deutschland reden hörtest?

d) ... er nach Deutschland kam, weil er mehr Deutsch lernen wollte.

e) ... er das Gefühl hatte, er würde die Deutschen nie verstehen, als er auf dem Flughafen in München ankam?

f) … er eine Gruppe von Bayern beobachtete, die sich über etwas unterhielten, was er nicht verstehen konnte?

……

……

g) … Josh eine Weile stehen blieb und daran dachte, sofort nach Hause zu fliegen?

……

……

h) … er jedoch in Deutschland blieb und viele Freunde gewann?

……

……

i) … er sich schon darauf freut wieder in seine Heimat zurückzukehren, obwohl er viele Freunde gefunden hat?

……

……

j) … seine Gastfamilie ohne Zögern zusagte, als sie gefragt wurde, ob sie ihn in den USA besuchen wollten?

……

……

Reported speech (indirect speech)

REGEL: Man verwendet die **indirekte Rede**, um zu berichten, was jemand gesagt oder geschrieben hat. Da sich die Sprecherperspektive ändert, müssen bei einem Text, der von der direkten in die indirekte Rede gesetzt wird, einige Änderungen vorgenommen werden, z. B. bei Pronomen und Possessivbegleiter, bei Adverbialbestimmungen und vor allem bei den Tempora. Die Zeiten der direkten Rede werden in der indirekten Rede um eine Zeitstufe in die Vergangenheit verschoben.

Backshift of tenses

direct speech	reported / indirect speech
simple present	simple past
present progressive	past progressive
present perfect	past perfect
simple past	past perfect
past perfect	past perfect bleibt

direct speech	reported / indirect speech
will-future	would + infinitiv e
going-to future	was / were going to + infinitive
can	could
may	might

Aussagesätze werden in der indirekten Rede mit Verben eingeleitet wie z. B. ***agree, answer, know, point out, remark, say, tell s. o., think etc.***

Nick: "John is my best friend!" → Nick said (that) John was his best friend.
May: "I will travel to Florida." → May told us (that) she would travel to Florida.

Fragesätze werden in der indirekten Rede mit Verben wie ***ask, want to know, wonder*** etc. eingeleitet. Wenn die direkte Rede mit einem Fragewort beginnt, wird dieses auch in der indirekten Rede übernommen. Bei Fragen ohne Fragewort verwendet man ***if*** oder ***whether***.

David: "What do you like to eat?" → David asked what she liked to eat.
David: "Do you like peas?" → David asked whether she liked peas.

Zeitangaben der direkten Rede, die am selben Tag, im selben Monat oder Jahr in indirekter Rede wiedergegeben werden, werden übernommen. Wird aber zu einem späteren Zeitpunkt berichtet, verändern sie sich folgendermaßen:

direct speech	reported / indirect speech
today	that day
now	then
tomorrow	the next / following day
tonight	that night
this week / month / year	that week / month / year
next week / month / year	the next / following week / month / year
last week / year / Saturday	the week / year / Saturday before
two days ago	*two days before*

9 **Convert the following sentences into reported speech. Use different introductory verbs. Start like this: He said ...**

a) I am going to Dublin for the U2 Concert.

....

b) I am not just seeing the band, I'm helping with the show.

....

c) I will be helping set up the stage and the light show.

....

d) It is an amazing thing and I can't believe it is happening to me.

....

e) I was following the band throughout Europe on their last tour.

....

f) In just under two weeks, I saw them 10 times in 10 different cities.

....

....

g) At every concert, I managed to get front row seats, although sometimes they were really expensive.

....

....

h) After the eighth show, Bono told me that he had seen me too many times and that I should join the road crew for the tour.

....

....

i) I am still going to University next year, but now I'm enjoying an experience of a lifetime.

....

....

10 **Now convert these questions into reported speech.**

a) Bono, when did you give your first concert?

....

b) How did U2 become successful in Ireland?

....

c) Had you ever thought of becoming famous before your success?

....

d) Have you got enough time for friends despite your job?

....

e) What are your plans for the next years?

....

f) Do you think you will still be on stage in 10 years?

....

g) Can you imagine doing any other job?

....

h) Have you ever been disappointed after a concert?

....

REGEL: Befehle (*imperatives*), Bitten oder Ratschläge werden in der indirekten Rede mit einem einleitenden Verb wie ***ask, forbid, order, persuade, remind, request, tell, warn*** etc. eingeleitet. Der Befehl wird durch ***should*** oder den Infinitiv mit ***to*** ausgedrückt.

Rita: "Please, be quiet now!"

→ Rita said they should be quiet. → Rita asked them to be quiet.

11 Convert these commands and requests of a concerned mother into reported speech.

a) Don't buy a new CD every week.

....

b) Tell me when you intend to go to a concert.

....

c) Don't spend the night with people you don't know.

....

d) Take a taxi home if the concert ends very late.

....

e) Bring me an autograph of my favourite singer.

....

Passive voice

REGEL: Das **Aktiv** hebt hervor, wer oder was eine Handlung vornimmt. Das **Passiv** hingegen hebt hervor, was mit einer Person oder Sache geschieht. Dabei ist meist unwichtig, wer oder was diese Handlung ausführt. Das Passiv lässt sich von allen Verben bilden, die im Aktiv ein direktes Objekt nach sich ziehen (transitive Verben). Es wird mit einer Form von ***be*** + Partizip Perfekt (dritte Verbform) gebildet.

Right-hand driven Volkswagen cars are made in South Africa.
Coffee and cake have been served in the living room.
Money can be exchanged here.

Zeit	Passiv
Simple present	*Most T-shirts are made of cotton*
Present progressive	*A new swimming pool is being built.*
Simple past	*The new gym was opened in 2005.*
Past progressive	*While the motorway was being reconstructed there were a lot of traffic jams.*
Present perfect	*Up to now a lot of trees have been cut down.*
Past perfect	*The cars were sold after they had been repaired.*
Will-future	*You will be told when the next test takes place.*
Going-to-future	*The new playground is going to be finished in two weeks.*
Infinitive (auxiliary or substitute + be + past participle)	*The main door should always be closed.*
Imperativ (Lock the classroom at all times after school.)	*The classroom is to be locked at all times after school.*

Bei Verben, die im Aktiv mit einem direkten und einem indirekten Objekt verbunden sind (wie z. B. ***ask, give, offer, pay, promise, send, show, teach, tell, write***), wird meistens das **indirekte Objekt als Subjekt des Passivsatzes** verwendet.

Aktiv	dir. Obj.	indir. Obj.	Passiv
Someone gave	*him*	*the key.*	*He was given the key.*
		selten:	*The key was given to him.*

Ausnahmen:
Bei den Verben ***describe, explain, introduce, mention, say*** und ***suggest*** muss das indirekte Objekt immer mit **to** angeschlossen werden.
The cartoon is described to me.* Nicht: *~~I am~~ described the cartoon.
Wenn der Handelnde im Passivsatz explizit genannt werden soll, schließt man ihn mit dem sogenannten *by-agent* an.

The school report was signed by the student's parents.

Bei Verben mit Präpositionen (z. B. ***ask for, laugh at, speak about, talk about, think of,*** etc.) folgt die Präposition wie im Aktiv direkt dem Verb.

The children talked about the problem. → The problem was talked about.

12 Here is a list of some of the school rules at Laura's school. Change them into the passive voice, where possible.

a) Enter the school by the south doors only. We lock all the other doors until morning classes are over.

b) We do not allow running in the halls.

c) The school secretary keeps a set of keys for all classrooms.

d) Students in charge of extra curricular activities must lock all classrooms before they leave the building.

e) Do not damage school property.

f) You must wear non-marking running shoes in the gym.

g) You should use your lockers for personal belongings.

h) We expect you to be on time for your classes. Latecomers must sign in at the principal's office.

i) If you are late three times, we send a letter to your parents.

j) The school board will suspend any student caught cheating in an exam.

k) If a teacher has given a student a red notice, he or she must have his parents sign it.

13 Kevin is worried about his job interview and talks to his friend Sam who is more experienced. Fill in the blanks with suitable passive constructions.
Look for signal words to help you with the tenses.

Example: Kevin: What do you think I should wear for my interview next Monday? Does the way a person dresses influence employers?
Sam: A jacket and tie, at least. Employers are always influenced by the way a person dresses.

a) Kevin: Will more than one person ask me questions during the interview?

Sam: I'm sure you .... questions by a panel of interviewers.

b) Kevin: What kind of questions can I expect?

Sam: Questions on your family background, schooling, past work experience and general interests ....

c) Kevin: They are interviewing Petra today. We must find out how it goes.

Sam: That's right, she ....

d) Kevin: Have they ever conducted more than one interview for such a position?

Sam: Oh yes, more than one interview .... on several occasions.

e) Kevin: I heard that last year they really put applicants to the test.

Sam: Not just last year, but the year before as well, applicants .... through the wringer.

f) Kevin: Did you hear about Jack? Two weeks ago while he .... interviewed, someone from personnel interrupted and called off the whole thing. Apparently when they double-checked his application form, he hadn't fulfilled all their requirements.

I find that unprofessional, don't you?

Sam: I guess so, but some of the employees in personnel .... (to be put under pressure) and so documents .... (not double-check) thoroughly. Rules are rules, though, and requirements .... (have to fulfil), otherwise it's not fair to other applicants.

g) Kevin: How about if we do a mock interview and you can tell me what I need to work on?

Sam: Certainly. I'll try my best to tell you what needs ....

Conditional sentences

REGEL: Bedingungssätze bestehen aus einem Hauptsatz und einem *if*-Satz (in beliebiger Reihenfolge). Man drückt damit aus, was unter bestimmten Bedingungen geschieht, geschehen könnte oder geschehen wäre.

Man unterscheidet drei Typen von Bedingungssätzen:

Typ I: Erfüllbare Bedingung
Wenn eine Bedingung realistisch und erfüllbar ist, benutzt man im ***if-clause*** das ***simple present***, im Hauptsatz das ***will***-Futur:

If I do ***my homework every day,*** → ***I*** *will pass* ***the test.***
He *will go* ***to the dance lesson*** → *if* ***you*** *join* ***him.***

Typ II: Unwahrscheinliche oder nicht erfüllbare Bedingung
Wenn eine Bedingung unrealistisch ist oder nicht den Tatsachen entspricht, benutzt man im ***if-clause*** das ***simple past***, im Hauptsatz das ***conditional***:

If ***you*** *weren't* ***so mean all the time,*** → ***I*** *would help* ***you.***
She *would buy* ***more clothes*** → *if* ***she*** *had* ***the money.***

Typ III: Unmögliche Bedingung
Diesen Typ verwendet man, wenn eine Bedingung keinesfalls erfüllt werden kann, weil sie sich auf die Vergangenheit bezieht. Im ***if-clause*** steht das ***past perfect***, im Hauptsatz das ***conditional perfect***:

If ***I*** *had known* ***you then,*** → ***I*** *would have married* ***you.***
We *wouldn't have had* ***cramps*** → *if* ***we*** *hadn't eaten* ***so much.***

14 Complete the conditional sentences. Pay attention to the correct tenses.

a) My mum wouldn't complain about my marks at school if I .... my homework regularly. (do)

b) If I get my driver's licence, I .... you home every day. (drive)

c) If we .... by bus instead of using the car all the time, we could do something to save our environment. (go)

d) Some people say there will be another nuclear accident like the one in Fukushima if we .... using nuclear energy. (go on)

e) If I .... so much about environmental problems, I wouldn't have started sorting our waste some years ago. (not learn)

15 Underline the correct solution.

a) If John doesn't play football this season, the school team (will lose/would lose/would have lost) the championship.
b) More members would show up at our photography club meetings if we (make/would make/made) them more interesting.
c) I won't be angry if you (tell/told/will tell) the truth.
d) If drug dealers didn't exploit teenagers at clubs, they (might not/will not/wouldn't have) become addicts.
e) Writing letters the old-fashioned way may become obsolete if more people (would send/sent/sended) e-mails.
f) The orchestra wouldn't know how fast to play a piece if the conductor (didn't direct/wouldn't direct/hadn't directed) them properly.
g) Computer technology will expand even more if progress (continued/continues/will continue).
h) If you (have had/would have had/had had) more time, you could have helped me.
i) "Olivia and Raphael, you may not go swimming if you both (don't stop/won't stop/didn't stop) fighting right now!"
j) Do you think Sam (will go/would have gone/would go) to the dance with me if I had asked him.

★ **16 You spent a disastrous holiday with a friend in Paris. You wish things had worked out differently. Tell another friend, Laura, in an e-mail about how you feel. Use the ideas below. Try to make your e-mail sound as authentic as possible (using conditional type III). The expressions below may help you with your writing. Remember to write an appropriate ending. If you are not sure about your e-mail, ask your teacher for help.**

Janet very bossy/not relaxed	I tried too hard to please her
Janet chose expensive hotel	we had no money for fun
Janet took bus everywhere	I enjoy just wandering around and discovering new things
Janet found metro too dangerous and thought we'd get robbed at flea market	we didn't go to flea market
Janet insisted on daily itineraries	fun to buy food at markets and eat outdoors; Janet had higher budget
Janet made no attempt to speak any French	I spoke French even if it didn't sound good
Janet went to bed at 9 pm	I ended up going out at night alone
Janet unwilling to try North African food	I love couscous

wait till you hear this • you won't belive it • like you always say • the awful thing • I really need to be more assertive • by the way • also • oh well • sorry I've dumped this on you • ...

Zwischentest

3

1 **Find an example of the active and another one of the passive in the same paragraph of the text "Girls and Guitars" (p. 25) and write down how the passive is formed.**

active: ....

....

....

passive: ....

....

....

2 **Using the prompts below to form passive sentences.**

a) Bob Dylan – regard – one of the most important musicians of rock and pop music

....

....

b) famous songs like "Knockin' On Heaven's Door" and "Like A Rolling Stone" – write – Bob Dylan

....

....

c) "Blowin' In The Wind" – one of his first hits – write – in the 1960s

....

....

d) first rock double album "Blonde On Blonde" – release – 1966

....

....

e) song "Hurricane" from the album Desire – record – 1975 – release – 1976

....

....

f) other singers and musicians like REM, U2 and Sheryl Crow – influence – by him

....

....

g) at the beginning of the 21st century – award – Oscar – for his composition "Things Have Changed"

....

....

h) surely – his songs – hear, play, sing – in the future

....

....

8

3 **Read the following sentences and analyse the marked parts in the sentences. Say what forms of the verb they are. Rewrite sentences a) and b) using other structures.**

a) Five years ago in the US, Tish Ciravolo, a bass guitar player, set up the first company to produce guitars made for girls.
b) Tish says, "What I wanted to do was not only design a guitar for a girl to play, but to change the consciousness – make the sight of a girl playing the guitar as natural as that of a girl playing the flute.
c) And, apart from just designing guitars that girls could play, I believed a guitar should be fun – I wanted them to be girlie – I wanted girls aged eight to 11 to say, 'Wow – I want to play!'"

3

4 **Now rewrite the sentences below using participle constructions.**

a) Last week Britney bought a guitar in a music shop in London. It was offered for £160.

....

....

b) She had watched the shop assistant. He had shown different flutes to a woman and her child.

....

....

c) After she had bought the new instrument she wanted to try it out immediately.

....

....

d) At the moment Britney is sitting in her bedroom. She is playing her new guitar.

....

....

4

5 Use relative clauses to explain the following things / terms.

a) piano b) concert

c) song d) guitarist

6 e) orchestra f) CD

6 What type of conditional clause is this?

If you can't, or don't have the money to pay for lessons, then you can use a book or just learn to play your favourite songs.

1 ....

★ **7 Put the sentence halves together. Write the correct letter next to each number below. You have to be familiar with all types of conditional sentences for this exercise. Then write down what type of conditional sentence they are.**

1. I would have been heartbroken
2. If Glen hadn't been ill for two weeks
3. If you visit us in Glasgow
4. I would eat more chocolate
5. If you meet Danny

A if I weighed less.
B please give him my love.
C if you had left me.
D he would have had better results.
E we will go to the Indian restaurant.

....

....

....

....

....

....

....

....

....

5 ....

30 **Gesamtpunktzahl**

Kontrollieren Sie Ihre Ergebnisse mithilfe der Lösungen (S. 116/117) und addieren Sie die erreichten Punkte.

☐ 30 bis 24 Punkte: ☺ ☐ 23 bis 16 Punkte: 😐 ☐ 15 bis 0 Punkte: ☹

Sprachliche Mittel – 3

Vorschau
→ Word order/Inversion
→ Adjectives – Adverbs

Word order

REGEL: Einfache Aussagesätze werden im Englischen nach einem festen Muster zusammengesetzt:
Subjekt – Verb – restlicher Satz.

Dieses Muster verändert sich auch nicht, wenn dem Satz ein Nebensatz (Beispielsatz 1) oder eine adverbiale Bestimmung (Beispielsatz 2) vorangeht. (Bei mehreren aufeinanderfolgenden adverbialen Bestimmungen → siehe Satzstellung bei Adverbien, Seite 59). Auch wenn der direkten Rede ein Nachsatz mit Pronomen folgt, bleibt die Satzstellung erhalten (Beispielsatz 3).

		Subjekt	Verb	restlicher Satz
		Katharine	*loves*	*sports.*
1	*When school was over*	*my teacher*	*heard*	*all the children leaving.*
2	*Unfortunately*	*the tip*	*was*	*a disaster*
3	*„Can you bringt some food to the party?“ he asked.*			

Verneinte Sätze bildet man, indem man vor das Verb ein verneintes Hilfsverb stellt. Gibt es kein Hilfsverb in der Aussage, wird ***don't/doesn't*** oder ***didn't*** eingefügt.

Subjekt	vern. Hilfsverb	Verb	restlicher Satz
Tuan	*hasn't*	*seen*	*his latest film.*
Nick	*didn't*	*enjoy*	*the match.*

Fragen bildet man mithilfe eines Hilfsverbs. In Sätzen ohne Hilfsverb wird ***do/does/did*** verwendet.

Ausnahme: Wenn aber nach dem Subjekt eines Satzes gefragt wird, ist die Wortstellung **Fragewort – Verb – restlicher Satz.**

Fragewort	Hilfsverb	Subjekt	Verb	restlicher Satz
	Can	*you*	*speak*	*English?*
Where	*did*	*he*	*go*	*last night?*
Who			*helped*	*my daughter?*

1 Find the correct order of the words and phrases to form sentences.

a) the supermarket – in the evening – goes to – never – Ben

....

b) reading – spends – Kevin – often – a book – his afternoons – in the park

....

....

c) this wonderful town – has been living – now – Jenny – for – in – more than 12 years

....

....

d) went to – the new film – Alan – after – had seen – bed – he

....

e) the meeting – although – was – came to – Frank – ill – terribly – he

....

....

f) because – I – wanted to – phoned – where – the concert – my friend – was held – know – I

....

....

g) the new Tarantino film – the cinema – went to – see – they – in order to

....

....

h) was surfing – with our dog – I – my parents – the net – were taking a walk – while

....

....

i) fascinating – such – ever – you – have – seen – show – a?

....

j) the jacket – buy – where – did – I – so much – which – you – like?

....

....

2 The Millers, a family of four with their son Alec and their daughter Kate are on holiday in Spain. Ask questions about the underlined parts.

a) The Millers talked to the hotel manager.

....

b) They stayed in a 3 star beach hotel.

....

c) They arrived at 2 pm in the afternoon.

....

d) Alec has never been to Spain before.

....

e) The Millers are going to stay in Spain for two weeks.

....

f) Kate and Alec have to share a room because the hotel is too expensive.

....

g) Mrs Miller spent 50 € on her summer dress.

....

h) The Millers went to Spain by plane.

....

i) Kate discovered a spider in her bed.

....

j) Mr and Mrs Miller visited the most famous sights in Barcelona.

....

REGEL: Inversion

Werden am Anfang eines Satzes negative oder einschränkende adverbiale Bestimmungen verwendet, werden Subjekt und Hilfsverb umgestellt:

Not only was he successful in his job, but he had a happy family life, too.

Einschränkende/negative Adverbiale:

Hardly (... when), no sooner (... than) – kaum ..., als

Not only (..., but) – nicht nur, sondern auch

seldom, rarely – kaum/selten

neither/nor – weder noch

under no circumstances – unter keinen Umständen

at no time, never – niemals

3 Change the order of the sentences using inversion.

a) I had hardly come home when the storm started.

....

....

b) Taxes are not only annoying but also necessary.

....

....

c) The rules must not be broken under any circumstances.

....

....

d) He had never thought that he would win the lottery.

....

....

4 Complete the sentences using inversion in its correct tense.

Mary writes about her experiences in a hotel during her holidays to her cousin Isabel.

1. .... (I – never – be) in such an excellent hotel before.
2. .... (we – no sooner – arrive) at the hotel than the porter asked to take our luggage to our room.
3. However, ... (they – not only – look after) us in a very welcoming way, but the hotel's restaurant was also delicious.
4. .... (I – only later – find out) that the hotel is highly recommended by several web pages.

Modal auxiliaries

REGEL: ***Modal auxiliaries*** sind Verben, die nicht allein stehen können, sondern immer vor dem Infinitiv eines Vollverbs erscheinen. Sie erweitern dessen Bedeutung, indem sie eine Fähigkeit, eine Möglichkeit, eine Bitte oder Aufforderung zum Ausdruck bringen. ***Modal auxiliaries*** bilden nur ein oder zwei Zeiten, ansonsten werden ihre Ersatzformen (***substitutes***) benutzt.

Die folgende Liste gibt einen groben Überblick über die modalen Hilfsverben, ihre Ersatzformen und Verwendungen:

Hilfsverb	Ersatzform	Verwendung zum Ausdruck von	Beispiel
can/cannot	*(not) be able to (not) be allowed to*	Fähigkeit, Möglichkeit, Erlaubnis, Bitte	*I can sing well.*
could (not)		Fähigkeit, Möglichkeit, Erlaubnis in der Vergangenheit; Bitte	*He could not go to the concert because his parents didn't allow him to.*
may (not)	*(not) be allowed to*	Bitte um Erlaubnis, Möglichkeit	*You weren't allowed to come in then but you may come in now.*
might (not)		Möglichkeit, dass etwas geschieht	*There might be rain tomorrow.*
must (needn't)	*(not) have to*	Vorschrift, Notwendigkeit, Aufforderung	*A year ago she didn't have to work but now she must earn her own money.*
mustn't	*not be allowed to*	Verbot	*You mustn't smoke in here! It's prohibited!*
ought (not) to		(warnender) Ratschlag, Ermahnung	*He ought to call a lawyer.*
shall		Vorschlag, Angebot	*Shall we go out tonight?*
should (not)		Ratschlag	*I think you should apologize.*
will (won't)		höfliche Bitte oder Angebot	*Will you please help me?*
would (not)		höfliche Bitte oder Weigerung in der Vergangenheit	*Would you pass me the butter, please? They wouldn't let me in to the disco.*

★ **5** **Body Art has become increasingly popular over the past few years. More and more young people have piercings or tattoos because it makes them look "cool". It is important, however, to take certain precautions.**
Your best friend Sue has decided to have her lip pierced. Can you give her some advice?
Use the ideas below and the following modal auxiliaries or their substitutes: should, must, mustn't, have to, can, could, may, might.
Convince your friend of the importance of safety measures.

a) your shots/vaccinations up to date, especially for tetanus and hepatitis / save you trouble later on

....

....

b) shop around before deciding on a piercing shop

....

....

c) ensure piercer is qualified and experienced/check his/her portfolio/ piercer wears gloves

....

....

d) shop needs to be clean, safe and professional (an autoclave for sterilizing needles and other equipment is available)

....

....

e) if the area to be pierced not cleaned with the proper soap (antiseptic), lead to infection

....

....

f) the needle used is sterilized and clean

....

....

g) piece of jewellery sterilized before attached to body part

....

....

h) pierced area is cleaned

i) piercer gives specific instructions for post piercing care

j) know what steps to take if pierced area gets infected; perhaps this sounds too much, but all for your own good.

6 **Sarah will soon be going to Sydney/Australia on an exchange program. A lot of things will be different there for her. Form sentences in the future using substitutes for the auxiliaries.**

Beispiel: can choose between many extracurricular acitivities
Sarah will be able to choose between many …

a) must wear school uniform

b) cannot phone her friends every day

c) mustn't go barefoot in the grass because of spiders and snakes

d) needn't get up so early in the morning because school starts at 9 o'clock

e) must use sunscreen every day

f) can go surfing at the weekends

7 **Teenagers 50 years ago. Answer these questions about adolescents using the past tense. Look at the pictures to get some ideas.**

play computer games

work hard

go to the disco

go for a walk with their family on Sunday

use mobile phones

go to the cinema

a) What did they have to do every day? ....

....

b) What were they allowed to do at weekends? ....

....

c) What weren't they allowed to do every day? ....

....

d) What weren't they able to do? ....

....

Adjectives – adverbs

REGEL: Adjektive verwendet man, um zu beschreiben, wie jemand oder etwas ist.

He is a perfect friend. It was a wonderful day.

Adverbien werden häufig verwendet, um zu beschreiben, wie jemand etwas tut.
Es gibt aber auch Adverbien, die sich z.B. auf andere Adjektive, Adverbien oder ganze Sätze beziehen können.

He drives his new car carefully.
He is a very good driver. Actually, he has never had an accident.

Viele Adverbien der Art und Weise werden gebildet, indem man an das Adjektiv die Endung ***-ly*** anhängt, z.B. ***bad – badly, slow – slowly.***

Sonderregeln:

- Das Adverb zu ***good*** heißt ***well.***
- Das Adverb zu ***friendly*** heißt ***in a friendly way***.
- Das Adverb zu ***difficult*** heißt ***with difficulty***.
- Adjektiv und Adverb haben die gleiche Form: ***hard, fast, long, low.***
- Adverbien mit zwei Formen und unterschiedlicher Bedeutung:
  hard (hart) – ***hardly*** (kaum)
  pretty (ziemlich) – ***prettily*** (hübsch)
  fair (fair) – ***fairly*** (ziemlich)
  high (hoch) – ***highly*** (höchst)
  late (spät) – ***lately*** (in letzter Zeit)

Die Grundform von Adjektiven und Adverbien heißt „Positiv“. Wenn man Personen, Dinge, Zustände oder Tätigkeiten miteinander vergleicht, steigert man Adjektive und Adverbien, um Gleichheit oder Ungleichheit auszudrücken.
Einsilbige Adjektive und Adverbien oder zweisilbige Adjektive, die auf ***-er, -le, -ow, -y*** enden, werden mit ***-er*** (Komparativ) und ***-est*** (Superlativ) gesteigert.

nice – nicer – nicest, friendly – friendlier – friendliest.

Alle anderen zwei- und mehrsilbigen Adjektive und Adverbien werden mit ***more*** und ***most*** gesteigert:

beautiful – more beautiful – most beautiful
beautifully – more beautifully – most beautifully

Um **Gleichheit** auszudrücken, kann man ***as* – Positiv – *as*** verwenden, z.B. ***as cold as ice***. Um Ungleichheit auszudrücken, kann man ***not as* – Positiv – *as*** oder **Komparativ + *than*** verwenden:

not as cold as ice, not as beautiful as …
colder than ice, more beautiful than …

8 Put the adjectives and adverbs in the suitable form of the positive comparative or superlative.

a) (modern) In Canada the majority of high school students attend .... comprehensive schools than those existing in Germany.

b) (good) .... special needs programmes to assist weak students, high achievers, EFL language learners and even the handicapped etc. form an integral part of the curriculum.

c) (much) Unlike in Germany, students are not streamed after grade four. In Canada, they are given .... time to decide.

d) (little) .... pressure is placed on young learners to perform academically at such an early stage of their school career.

e) (bad) German schools are certainly not .... than Canadian ones – two countries, two systems.

f) (easy) (good) However, Canadian working parents find it .... than their German counterparts to organize child care. This is due to full-day schools as well as .... supervised after-school activities in Canada.

g) (extreme) (high) It is .... difficult for both parents to work in Germany. Classes generally end before lunch and places in after school centres (Hort) are .... coveted.

h) (good) (successful) Which is the .... school system of the two? A combination of both would probably be ....

i) (slow) When it comes to education, progress is often .... than one expects.

j) (important) (needed) The .... thing is to realize when reforms are .... and to ensure that pupils or students do not suffer from too much experimentation.

REGEL: Satzstellung von Adverbien

Je nachdem, auf welchen Satzteil sich Adverbien beziehen, stehen sie an verschiedenen Stellen innerhalb des Satzes. Sie stehen im Englischen jedoch niemals zwischen Verb und direktem Objekt:

He often buys new CDs. (nicht: He buys often new CDs.)

Satzadverbien stehen am Satzanfang:

Fortunately, we haven't had any problems.

Adverbien der Art und Weise stehen meist hinter dem Verb oder dessen Objekt, also am Satzende: ***He came home happily.***

Häufigkeitsadverbien stehen nach dem (ersten) Hilfsverb bzw. vor dem Vollverb:

We have never been to London.

Aber nach einer Form von ***be***, z. B. ***He is often late.***

Folgen mehrere adverbiale Bestimmungen aufeinander, so stehen sie in dieser Reihenfolge: **Art und Weise – Ort – Zeit:**

She walks slowly home in the afternoon.

9 Place the adverbs or adverbial phrases in the correct position in the sentences.

a) (mostly) In high school, overall grades are based on continuous assessment.

....

....

b) (generally) Students receive what is known as credits for subjects passed at the end of the year.

....

....

c) (by the end of grade twelve) In order to graduate from high school, one has to have accumulated the required number of credits.

....

....

d) (until now) University entrance grade requirements have varied depending on the course of study to be pursued.

....

....

e) (moreover) We do not have secondary school state exams equivalent to the "Realschulabschluss" or "Abitur," unlike the English with their nationwide O-levels (GCSE) and A-levels (advanced levels).

....

....

f) (seldom) High school students in Germany are given a second chance to rewrite final examinations which they fail.

g) (unfortunately) Canadian tertiary institutions have higher tuition costs than German ones.

h) (successfully) Students who have completed grade twelve can enter community college, polytechnic institutions or university.

i) (in Germany) (often) (at the age of 10) School children are placed under enormous pressure.

★ **10 Wie kannst du auf Englisch sagen, dass …**
(Achte dabei auf die korrekte Adverbposition.)

a) … verschiedene PISA-Studien zeigen, dass deutsche Schüler häufig nicht so gute Ergebnisse haben wie Schüler anderer europäischer Länder.

b) … leider nicht alle Schüler die Schule erfolgreich abschließen.

c) … man oft mehr motivierte Schüler an moderneren und besser ausgestatteten Schulen finden kann.

d) … dringend benötigte Reformen des Schulsystems in Deutschland ziemlich lange dauern.

Zwischentest

1 Complete the chart with the help of the text "Girls and Guitars" (page 25). Write down two ways of how we compare adjectives.

positive	comparative	superlative
famous	more famous	
light		lightest
narrow		narrowest
good	better	

4

2 Compare the given items.

a) a local politician – the German chancellor – the US President (powerful)
b) a gramophone – a record player – a CD-player (modern)
c) an autograph – an interview – a live concert (interesting)
d) a crossword puzzle – a test – an exam (difficult)

4

3 Find sentences with three different modal auxiliaries or their substitutes in the text "Girls and Guitars" (page 25).

3

4 Complete the chart.

modal auxiliaries	substitutes
	be able to
	be allowed to
must	

3

5 Fill in the gaps using modal auxiliaries and their substitutes.

a) As a child I .... go to my favourite bands' concerts.
b) But since I liked music a lot, I .... play simple songs on the guitar at the age of eight.
c) In order to learn how to play more musical instruments I .... attend music school twice a week.
d) Today I .... only play five different instruments, I also have my own band.

4

Gesamtpunktzahl 18

Kontrollieren Sie Ihre Ergebnisse mithilfe der Lösungen (S. 119) und addieren Sie die erreichten Punkte.

☐ 18 bis 14 Punkte: 🙂 ☐ 13 bis 9 Punkte: 😐 ☐ 8 bis 0 Punkte: 🙁

Referate

Vorschau

→ Grundlegendes und Nützliches zu Referat und *2-minute-speech*
→ Arbeitshilfe:
Checklist presentation

Im folgenden Kapitel wird Ihnen gezeigt, wie Sie effektiv präsentieren können (*2-minute-speech*, Buchvorstellung, Referat etc.).
2-minute-speeches unterscheiden sich von längeren Präsentationen nur darin, dass man kaum visuelle Materialien einsetzt (abgesehen von einer Landkarte oder einem Bild) und in zeitlich knapper Form die wichtigsten Fakten vermitteln muss.

Introduction/conclusion

REGEL: „Der erste Eindruck ist der wichtigste, der letzte Eindruck bleibt".
Einstieg und Schluss sind das Rückgrat Ihrer Präsentation. Während der ersten drei Sätze machen sich die Zuhörer ein Bild von Ihnen. Sie schätzen Stimme, Gestik und auch Art und Weise Ihres Redestils ab. Der Schluss rundet Ihre Präsentation ab und hinterlässt einen bleibenden Eindruck auf Ihre Zuhörer. Fehler im Mittelteil werden verziehen, wenn der Zuhörer das Gefühl hat, dass die Präsentation in sich stimmig und logisch geendet hat. Deshalb ist es wichtig, dass Sie diese beiden Teile besonders intensiv vorbereiten.

TIPP

DO'S and DON'TS

- ☺ Interessanter Einstieg und Ausklang, z. B. Musik, Cartoon, Bild, Zitat, Witz, lustige (aber themenbezogene) Anekdoten, überraschende Untersuchungsergebnisse, Einbeziehung der Zuhörer ...
- ☺ Es ist notwendig, das Thema Ihrer Präsentation nach dem Einstieg zu nennen.
- ☺ Anschließend müssen Sie Ihre Zuhörer über die Länge und die Hauptpunkte Ihrer Präsentation informieren. Das hilft dem Publikum, sich auf Ihren Vortrag einzustellen.
- ☺ Beenden Sie Ihre Präsentation nicht einfach, sondern fassen Sie zusammen, geben Sie einen Ausblick in die Zukunft, etc.
- ☹ ***„today I want to talk about ..."*** oder ***„My presentation is about ..."*** etc.
- ☹ ***„I hope you liked my presentation ..."*** oder ***„That's it ..."*** oder ***„Now I'm finished ..."***

Beispiel: „Statue of Liberty"
Einstieg:
„There is a lady in the United States of America who wears 8 meter long shoes.

This would be size 1200!"
Zusätzlich zum Einleitungssatz könnte man ein Bild als visuelle Unterstützung einsetzen.

Ausklang:
„However, Statues of Liberty cannot only be found in New York, but also in places all over the world."

1 **Look for a humorous introduction on the topic „Australia – a dangerous place to live"!**

2 **How could you start a presentation about Canada comparing the size of Canada and Germany?**

....

....

....

....

....

....

....

....

....

3 **Finish a presentation on the topic „Vampires – new superheroes" in an interesting way.**

....

....

....

....

....

....

....

....

....

Working with information

Es gibt verschiedene Quellen, auf die Sie bei Ihrer Recherche zurückgreifen können. Neben dem Internet haben Sie z. B. die Möglichkeit, die Bibliothek Ihrer Schule/Stadt zu besuchen oder Zeitschriften und Zeitungen zu verwenden. Jedoch gibt es bei der Verarbeitung von Informationen einige Punkte, die Sie unbedingt beachten müssen:

TIPP

DO'S and DON'TS

- ☺ Vereinfachen Sie Originaltexte so weit, dass Ihre Klassenkameraden Ihrer Präsentation ohne Einsatz von Dolmetschern folgen können!
- ☺ Unbekannte Wörter (max. 10) müssen Sie während Ihres Referates erklären und eventuell schriftlich präsentieren (z. B. Tafel, Folie, Handout). Prüfen Sie zuvor die richtige Aussprache.
- ☺ Informationen müssen logisch aufeinander aufbauen. Übernehmen Sie diese nicht nur, um sie dann aneinanderzureihen.
- ☹ Stützen Sie sich bei Ihrer Recherche nicht nur auf Wikipedia®, sondern nutzen Sie ein breites Spektrum an Quellen.
- ☹ Übernehmen Sie Texte/Textteile aus den Quellen nur in begründeten Ausnahmefällen wörtlich. Kennzeichnen Sie dann diese Zitate. Grundsätzlich ist es Ihre Aufgabe, eigenständig zu formulieren. Zudem sind fremdsprachliche Originaltexte meist zu schwierig.
- ☹ Langweilen Sie Ihre Zuhörer nicht mit einer Aneinanderreihung von Zahlen und Ereignissen. Besonders geschichtliche oder personenbezogene Themen verleiten dazu.

4 Underline the most important information in the excerpt about Rosa Parks and rewrite it in your own words.

Rosa Parks Biography

Pioneer of Civil Rights

Rosa Parks Date of birth: February 4, 1913
Date of death: October 24, 2005
Most historians date the beginning of the modern civil rights movement in the United States to December 1, 1955. That was the day when an unknown seamstress in Montgomery, Alabama refused to give up her bus seat to a white passenger. This brave woman, Rosa Parks, was arrested and fined for violating a city ordinance, but her lonely act of defiance began a movement that ended legal segregation in America, and made her an inspiration to freedom-loving people everywhere.

http://www.achievement.org/autodoc/page/par0bio-1

Using media

Der funktionierende und sinnvolle Einsatz von Medien ist von entscheidender Bedeutung. Typische Medien, die Sie in der Schule verwenden können, sind:
- Tafel
- Overheadprojektor
- CD-/DVD-Player
- Bilder/Plakate/Fotos/Prospekte/Gegenstände
- Computer and Beamer (digitale Präsentation)

Wichtig ist, dass die Medien Ihre Informationen unterstützen und nicht zum Selbstzweck eingesetzt werden.
Das Motto für den Medieneinsatz muss lauten: Alles, was sinnvoll ist; nichts, damit es lediglich benutzt wird.

Beachten Sie:

TIPP

DO'S and DON'TS

☺ Tafel: Schreiben Sie die notwendigen Informationen leserlich, gut strukturiert und vor allem **vor** Ihrer Präsentation an die Tafel.

☺ Overhead: die Qualität der Folien ist entscheidend (gut lesbare Schrift, Absätze, Bildauflösung und -größe und eventuell Farbe).
Viele Schulen haben keinen Farbkopierer; deshalb müssen Sie sich eventuell vorzeitig und andernorts um die Erstellung von farbigen Folienkopien kümmern.

☺ CD-/DVD-Player: Überprüfen Sie vorher, ob die Geräte reserviert werden müssen und ob sie funktionstüchtig sind! Der Aufbau muss **vor** der Präsentation abgeschlossen sein.

☺ Fotos: Sollten Sie viele Fotos verwenden, bietet sich eine Computerpräsentation an, bei wenigen Bildern eignen sich Folien besser.

☹ Schauen Sie bei Ihrer Ausführungen nicht die Medien, sondern Ihre Zuhörer an. Der Kontakt zum „Zielpublikum" verbessert dessen Aufmerksamkeit.

☹ Keine Medienschlacht. Nicht die Quantität, sondern die Qualität zählt. Das Motto kann auch hier lauten: ***Less is more.***

☹ Geben Sie Bilder, Prospekte oder Gegenstände nicht während Ihrer Präsentation zur Ansicht herum. Das lenkt ihre Zuhörer ab und vermindert so deren Aufmerksamkeit.

☹ Verdecken Sie die Medien nicht, indem Sie sich vor diese stellen.
Da man Sie aber trotzdem sehen soll, ist der beste Platz neben den Medien.

☹ Überfordern Sie Ihre Zuhörer nicht durch zu schnelle Wechsel.
Lassen Sie ihnen genügend Zeit, sich z. B. Bilder in Ruhe anzusehen.

Using your PC

Computergestützte Präsentationen (z. B. mit PowerPoint®) sind ein beliebtes Mittel, das viele Vorteile bietet, aber auch durch falschen Einsatz zum Scheitern der Präsentation führen kann.

TIPP

DO'S and DON'TS

- Sie müssen unbedingt **vor** Ihrem Vortrag die Präsentation auf dem Schulcomputer ausprobieren oder Ihren eigenen Computer mitbringen.
  Oft wird ein Dateiformat nicht erkannt oder Filme/Audiodateien können nicht abgespielt werden.
- Eine Fernbedienung hilft Ihnen bei Ihrer Präsentation sehr.
  Haben Sie keine, kann Ihnen ein Mitschüler/eine Mitschülerin beim Weiterklicken als Helfer dienen. So werden Sie selbst nicht abgelenkt.
- Es kann Ihnen helfen, wenn der Computer vor Ihnen steht, sodass Sie Ihre Präsentation im Blick haben, ohne immer an die Wand schauen zu müssen.
- Jeder neue Aspekt bekommt seine eigene Seite bzw. digitale Folie. Denken Sie immer an eine visuelle Unterstützung/Merkhilfe. Übertreiben Sie dabei nicht.
- Kümmern Sie sich um einen Ersatzplan, falls die Medien aus technischen Gründen nicht funktionieren sollten, z. B. die Seiten ausdrucken, zusätzliches Speichern auf Memory-Stick und CD.
- Verwenden Sie nicht zu viele verschiedene Farben und Animationen.
- Wählen Sie keine zu kleine Schriftgröße (mind. 20 pt) oder zu helle Farben bei der Schrift. Sie bieten keinen guten Kontrast zwischen Schrift und Hintergrund. Regel: in hellen Räumen heller Hintergrund mit dunkler Schrift, in dunklen Räumen dunkler Hintergrund mit heller Schrift.
- Verwenden Sie Schriftarten, die nicht verspielt sind oder zu dünne Striche haben: Diese sind nur auf Papier gut lesbar.
- Lange Texte haben in einer Computerpräsentationen nichts zu suchen.
  Verwenden Sie diese, um eine visuelle Unterstützung zu geben, nicht um Texte zu präsentieren. Verwenden Sie nur Schlagwörter und keine vollständigen Sätze. Längere Aufzählungen sollten Sie vermeiden. Sie sind für den Zuhörer langweilig. Lesen Sie nicht einfach vor, was auf der Folie gelesen werden kann. Sagen Sie das Gleiche in anderen Worten, dann vermeiden Sie Langeweile.
- Rechtschreib-, Zeichen- oder Grammatikfehler in den Texten sind zu vermeiden. Falls Sie sich nicht sicher sind, nutzen Sie bitte ein Wörterbuch und/oder zeigen Sie die Präsentation vorher Ihrer Lehrerin bzw. Ihrem Lehrer.

5 **A friend of yours is preparing a digital presentation about the "Statue of Liberty".**
He shows you one of the pages. Try to improve his work.

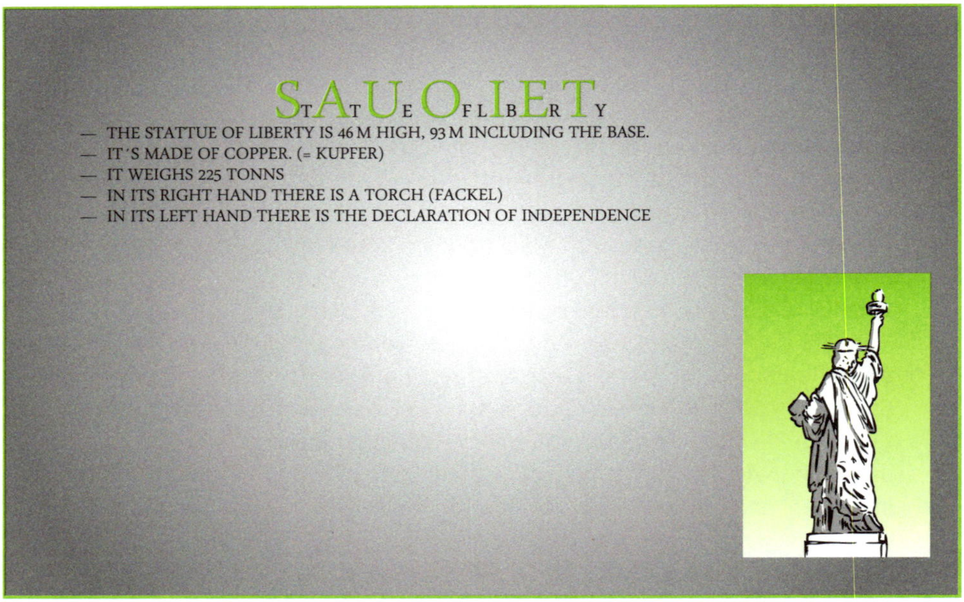

The presentation itself

Eine erfolgreiche Präsentation ist immer mit einer sorgfältigen Vorbereitung verbunden. Das bedeutet, dass Sie Ihre Präsentation zuvor **mehrmals geübt** haben. Sie sollten dabei die Zeit stoppen, damit Sie wissen, wie lange sie insgesamt dauert. Dies gibt Ihnen Sicherheit und hilft Ihnen, sich auf das Wesentliche zu konzentrieren.

Während der Präsentation gibt es einige Regeln, die Sie beachten sollten:

REGEL:

- Augenkontakt mit dem Publikum ist wichtig. Stellen Sie sich vor, Sie reden mit Freunden. Dies verleiht Ihnen Natürlichkeit.
- Reden Sie klar sowie deutlich und vergessen Sie nicht, beim Reden Pausen zu machen. Atmen ist erlaubt.
- Die Hände sind bei einer Präsentation manchen ein Problem. Sie gehören weder in die Hosentasche, noch verschränkt vor die Brust. Eine Fernbedienung oder kleine Karteikarten in der Hand zu halten, kann helfen.
- Eine digitale Präsentation oder andere Medien ersetzen Ihren Vortrag nicht. **Sie** sind die Hauptperson und stehen im Vordergrund.
- Eine spritzige und mit Elan vorgetragene Präsentation sichert Ihnen das Interesse des Publikums und lenkt zudem von Fehlern ab. Nichts ist schlimmer, als den Eindruck zu vermitteln, dass man die Präsentation nur macht, damit man sie hinter sich hat.
- Ihre Präsentation muss frei gehalten werden, d. h. reines Ablesen von (digitalen) Folien oder Notizkarten darf nicht sein. Auch das Auswendiglernen trägt nicht zu einer authentischen Rede bei. Wenn Sie gut vorbereitet sind, werden Sie keine Probleme haben, die richtigen Worte zu finden.

6 **Complete the following checklist for your next presentation in English.**

CHECKLIST

Introduction / conclusion

- ☐ interessanter Einstieg: z. B. ....

  ....
- ☐ ....

  ....
- ☐ ....

  ....
- ☐ ....

  ....

Working with information

- ☐ andere Quellen außer Wikipedia®, z. B. ....
- ☐ ....
- ☐ ....
- ☐ ....

Using media

- ☐ ....
- ☐ ....
- ☐ ....
- ☐ ....
- ☐ ....

Länge: .... Minuten

Geübt: .... Mal

Welche Geräte reserviert und überprüft: ....

Plan B für Medien: ....

Zwischentest

1 **Beschreiben Sie den Unterschied zwischen einer *2-minute-speech* und einer *presentation*.**

....

.... 2

2 **Bewerten Sie die beiden Einführungen in das Thema „National Parks of the United States".**

a) Good morning everybody. Today we play the game "what am I". I'm going to give you hints about the topic of my presentation. The first person who guesses right wins the game. Listen carefully.
- I exist all over the world.
- In the USA there are 58 of my kind.
- I cover about 210,000 square kilometers.
- Many people come to visit me.
- Sometimes fire can be dangerous to me.
- One of my names is Yellowstone.

b) Good morning everybody. My presentation is about the National Parks of the United States. There are 58 national parks in the USA today. I want to talk about a special national park: the Yellowstone National Park.

....

....

.... 4

3 **Nennen Sie fünf Möglichkeiten, eine Präsentation in gelungener Art und Weise einzuleiten.**

....

....

.... 5

4 **Was müssen Sie vor Ihrer Präsentation abklären/organisieren?**

....

....

.... 5

Gesamtpunktzahl **16**

Kontrollieren Sie Ihre Ergebnisse mithilfe der Lösungen (S. 120/121) und addieren Sie die erreichten Punkte.

☐ 16 bis 13 Punkte: ☺ ☐ 12 bis 8 Punkte: 😐 ☐ 7 bis 0 Punkte: ☹

Lesen

Vorschau

→ Informationen entnehmen
→ Inhalt erfassen
→ Texte verstehen

Informative texts / factual texts

TIPP

Kaum etwas stärkt das Sprachverständnis und die Vertrautheit mit der fremden Kultur so sehr wie der Umgang mit der Literatur. Das anfängliche Gefühl der Überforderung schwindet rasch, denn grundsätzlich gilt, dass man zum Verständnis von Texten nicht jedes Wort verstehen muss. Vieles lässt sich durch den Kontext erraten. Selbst wenn man sich bei der Übersetzung eines Begriffs nicht ganz sicher ist, wird man zumeist verstehen, worum es in dem Text geht.
Kommt es dem Leser darauf an, schnell die Hauptaussage eines Textes zu verstehen, verwendet man die sogenannte ***Skimming*-Technik** (***reading for gist***). Hierzu überfliegt man den Text, ohne dabei jedes einzelne Wort verstehen zu müssen. Allein wenn man die wichtigsten Wörter eines Satzes verstanden hat (Subjekt, Prädikat, Objekt), erfasst man die Hauptaussage des Textes. Diese Technik wendet man z. B. an, wenn man einen Zeitungsartikel schnell verstehen möchte.
Anders ist es beim sogenannten ***Scanning***. Auch hierbei wird ein Text zügig gelesen, jedoch um gezielt bestimmte Informationen zu entnehmen (***reading for detail***). Sofern möglich, markieren Sie am besten die Schlüsselwörter (***keywords***). Scanning bietet sich z. B. an, wenn man einen Fahrplan oder Informationsbroschüren liest, bei der nur bestimmte Teile für den Leser von Interesse sind.
Bei allen Texten, ob fiktional oder nicht-fiktional, sollte man darauf achten, warum und für wen sie geschrieben wurden. Häufig wird nämlich nicht offen (explizit) gesagt, welche Haltung der Autor zu dem Thema hat. Auch Nachrichten enthalten häufig neben den reinen Fakten implizite und damit interpretierende Aussagen, die bereits Stellung zum Thema beziehen und somit den Leser beeinflussen. Deshalb muss der Leser auf diese impliziten Äußerungen (***underlying message***) achten.

Newspaper article

Michael Jackson

Jan. 30, 2010

Michael Joseph Jackson's story was a quintessentially American tale of celebrity and excess that took him from musical boy wonder to global pop superstar to sad figure haunted by lawsuits, paparazzi and failed plastic surgery.

At the height of his career, he was indisputably the biggest star in the world; he has sold more than 750 million albums. He spent a lifetime surprising people, in recent years largely because of a surreal personal life, shocking scandals, serial plastic surgeries and eccentric public behavior that have turned him – on his very best days – into the target of late-night talk-show jokes and tabloid headlines. He died at age 50 in Los Angeles on June 25, 2009.

Mr. Jackson's death itself became an enormous spectacle. On television and on the Internet, tens of millions of people worldwide watched a memorial service at the Staples Center in Los Angeles.

The cause of Mr. Jackson's death was a mixture of powerful pills and drugs, according to the Los Angeles County Coroner office. The manner of death was determined to be homicide. Mr. Jackson's personal doctor, Conrad Murray, who tried to revive Mr. Jackson on the day he died, is the focus of a murder investigation by the Los Angeles Police Department.

The introduction to Mr. Jackson's Rock and Roll Hall of Fame entry seemed apt as a global audience followed reports of his hospitalization and then death:

„Michael Jackson is a singer, songwriter, dancer and celebrity icon with a vast catalog of hit records and countless awards to his credit. Beyond that, he has influenced the world like few entertainers before or since. As a solo performer, he has enjoyed a level of superstardom previously known only to Elvis Presley, the Beatles and Frank Sinatra."

---

http://topics.nytimes.com/top/reference/timestopics/people/j/michael_jackson/index.html

TIPP

Wenn Sie in einem Text einen Satz nicht auf Anhieb verstehen, schauen Sie die umliegenden Begriffe an. Selbst wenn Ihnen keine Übersetzung für ein Wort oder einen Begriff einfällt, können Sie den Satz meistens aus seinem **Kontext** heraus verstehen. Manchmal geben auch die grammatischen Formen Aufschluss über die mögliche Bedeutung von Begriffen. Wenn Sie den Text aber auch nach mehrmaligem Lesen nicht verstehen, schlagen Sie die Wörter in einem Wörterbuch oder einem Online-Lexikon nach. Bei E-Readern oder Tablets kann oftmals direkt auf Wörterbücher zugreifen.

1 Language and Vocabulary: Find words in the text "Michael Jackson" (page 73) which have the same meaning as the following words.

adequate		Line
apart from that		Line
chased		Line
enormous		Line
murder		Line
without any doubt		Line

2 Create a fact sheet about Michael Jackson using the most important information from the text (page 73).

Michael Jackson

✝ ....

Age: ....

Albums sold: ....

....

....

....

....

....

....

....

....

....

....

....

....

REGEL: How to answer questions on the text

- Ihre Aufgabe: Suchen Sie im Text die Stelle, zu der die Frage gestellt wird, und beantworten Sie diese in eigenen Worten.
- Im Text finden Sie oft eine sprachlich anspruchsvolle Form, die Sie z. B. vereinfachen, umschreiben oder erklären können.
- Wortschatz: Sie sollten nicht nur zeigen, dass Sie den Text verstehen, sondern auch eine gute sprachliche Ausdrucksweise demonstrieren.
  - Vermeiden Sie Wiederholungen ***(and … and … and).***
  - Verwenden Sie keinen eintönigen Verben ***(do, have, get, be).***
  - Vermeiden Sie Ausdrücke wie ***and things like that*** oder ***and so on.***
  - Zeitstufe: Übernehmen Sie die Zeitstufe aus der Frage und wechseln Sie nicht zwischen ***past***, ***present*** und ***future***.
- Keine eigene Meinung oder Vorwissen zum Thema einbringen. Bleiben Sie am Text.

★ **3** **Answer the following question in complete sentences.**
Try to use your own words as much as possible.

Explain why Michael Jackson is such an ambivalent character?

....

....

....

....

....

....

....

....

....

....

....

....

....

....

....

....

Extract from a travel guide

TIPP

Reiseführer
Sicher haben Sie schon einmal einen Reiseführer gelesen. Ist Ihnen dabei aufgefallen, dass die meisten Führer gut gegliederte Texte haben, die es dem Reisenden erleichtern, Informationen schnell zu finden?
Die Verfasser von Reiseführern haben bestimmte Zielgruppen im Auge.
Natürlich passen sie die Sprache entsprechend der Leserschaft an. Der folgende Auszug stammt aus einem Reiseführer für Rucksacktouristen.

SYDNEY, AUSTRALIA

Population: 3,700,000
As Australia's oldest and largest city, Sydney ("Sinney" to the locals) has plenty to offer.
Because Sydney grew in a **piecemeal** fashion, it has a tighter, more congested centre.
It's also a dazzlingly modern city, with the most energy and style in Australia.
The stupendous harbour, though, is more than just the centrepiece for the city, everything in Sydney revolves around it. Would the Opera House, for example, be anything like the place it is, if it wasn't **perched** right beside the harbour?

City Views

Sydney is becoming a mini-Manhattan and from up top you can look down on the **convoluted** streets.
Highest is the Sydney Tower on top of the Centrepoint complex on Market St.
This gigantic column has a viewing gallery and revolving restaurants on the summit, 305 metres above street level.
The Harbour Bridge is a good **vantage point** and you can climb the 200 stairs inside for panoramic views of the harbour and city.
Mrs Macquarie's Point, a **headland** east of the Opera House, has been a lookout since at least 1810 when Elizabeth Macquarie, wife of the governor, had a stone chair hewn into the rock, from where she would watch for ships entering the harbour.

Sydney Opera House

Whether you're at a free Sunday concert or sitting in the open-air restaurant watching the harbour life, the Opera House is a truly memorable place.
It has four auditoriums and puts on dance, theatre, concerts and films as well as opera.
Popular performances sell out quickly but there are often 'restricted view' tickets available. There are often free lunch hour concerts and recitals.

Sydney Opera House

Darling Harbour
A small harbour transformed into a major tourist site, it is a recreation ground packed with restaurants, shops, as well as many tourist attractions. Among these are the Sydney Aquarium whose all-Australian inhabitants include river fish, Barrier Reef fish and coral gardens, and crocodiles. Two 'oceanarium' tanks, with sharks, rays and other big fish in one, and Sydney Harbour marine life in the other are **moored** in the harbour.
The Powerhouse Museum which covers the decorative arts, science and technology and social history can also be found in Darling Harbour. It's open from 10 am to 5 pm daily and an admission fee is charged (free on the first Saturday of the month).

Art Gallery of New South Wales
The art gallery has an excellent permanent display of Australian, European, Asian and tribal art. There are also temporary exhibits and special exhibitions. Admission is free but fees may apply for the latter (special exhibitions).

Parks
Centennial Park is Sydney's biggest park with running, cycling and horse tracks, duck ponds and barbecue sites.
Balls Head Reserve is located on the north shore of the harbour west of the Harbour Bridge. It is a pocket of bushland with great views of the harbour and old Aboriginal rock paintings and carvings. Some of the other numerous parks in Sydney are Hyde Park, Sydney Olympic Park, and the Royal Botanical Gardens which has a hop-on hop-off trackless train to get around the Gardens' highlights.

Beaches
Sydney's beaches are one of its greatest assets. There are harbour beaches and ocean beaches . Harbour beaches are sheltered and calm and generally smaller; ocean beaches often have good surf. Swimming is considered safe. Shark patrols operate through the summer and ocean beaches are netted to prevent shark attacks. Probably the best known beach in Sydney is Bondi with a selection of cheap accommodation and eating places. Other beaches in and around Sydney include Watsons Bay, Lady Bay, Tamarama, Manly, Curl Curl, and Narabeen. There's good diving from ocean beaches and shipwrecks to explore from boat dives. Canoeing, kayaking, sailing and, of course, surfing are popular water sports and readily available to tourists.

Places to Stay
There is a wide selection of accommodation including top range hotels, countless travellers' hostels, bed & breakfasts and camping facilities (generally a long way from town).

Entertainment and Eating Out
Sydney has an enormous range of eateries offering an equally impressive range of cuisines, a reflection of the country's ethnic diversity. For a **splurge**, consider Kable's or Doyle's. Otherwise the selection of mid-range to cheap eating places which offer snacks, main courses or full meals is easy to find.

Simply wandering around the city is entertainment in itself. Last minute tickets for various performances and shows around town can be obtained from Halftix. In addition there are nightclubs with a variety of music to suit most tastes, cinemas and spectator sports – Australians love their 'rugby' and 'cricket'.

piecemeal – one part at a time (piece by piece)
convoluted – complex
headland – point of high land jutting out to sea
splurge – spend money extravagantly
perched – placed, resting
vantage point – favourable position
to be moored – to be parked (for sea vessels)

4 Without reading the travel guide again, answer the following questions:

a) What general topics does the text contain?

....

....

b) Name three of the mentioned sights.

....

....

c) Name three kinds of places where you can stay overnight in Sydney.

....

....

5 Complete the following task using complete sentences.

a) What is considered Sydney's central point of interest?

....

....

b) Which other international cityscape is Sydney compared to?

....

....

c) What is the highest structure in Sydney?

....

....

d) If you wanted to go out to an expensive restaurant in Sydney, where would you go?

....

....

★ 6 **Complete these sentences. Use your own words where possible.**

a) There is an array of international restaurants in Sydney because ...

....

....

b) Shark nets are placed at ocean beaches to ...

....

....

c) It is hard to get tickets for popular performances at the Opera House, but ...

....

....

d) If you appreciate Aboriginal tribal art, you ...

....

....

e) Aboriginal rock paintings can ...

....

....

Literature / drama

In many of his plays, Shakespeare writes about how power or the thirst for power can cause people to commit heinous crimes which eventually lead to their downfall. In Macbeth the main character Macbeth is guilty of the above. In the final act of Shakespeare's tragedy, after Macbeth's fortune has worsened, his followers have deserted him and his wife has died, he speaks the following words. This type of speech spoken for the audience is known as a soliloquy. (= Selbstgespräch)

William Shakespeare

MACBETH

She should have died **hereafter**.
There would have been a time for such a word.
Tomorrow, and tomorrow, and tomorrow
Creeps in this **petty pace** from day to day,
To the last syllable of recorded time,
And all our yesterdays have lighted fools
The way to dusty death. Out, out brief candle!
Life's but a walking shadow, a poor player
That **struts** and **frets** his hour upon the stage
And then is heard no more. It is a tale
Told by an idiot, full of sound and **fury**,
Signifying nothing.

hereafter – in future
creeps – crawls
"petty pace" – here an expression used to mean insignificant / ridiculous tempo / time
struts – paces in a boastful manner
frets – complains or worries
fury – anger

William Shakespeare, Macbeth, Act 5 Scene 5

★ 7 Reading for Understanding – Read and answer the questions.

a) Make a list of all of the things Macbeth compares life to (all the metaphors used for life, 3 examples).
b) Who do you think the "She" at the beginning of Macbeth's speech refers to?
c) What is meant by "All our yesterdays"?
d) Describe the mood created by Macbeth's words. How does the character feel?
e) What is meant by life being full of "sound and fury"?
f) Why is the adjective "dusty" used to describe death?

8 Vocabulary – fill in the blanks in the grid.

Noun	Adjective
fury	
significance	
	recorded
	petty
fool	

Literature / novel

Sophie's World is a novel about the History of Philosophy. Jostein Gaarder was born in Oslo in 1952. Sophie's World, the first of his books to be published in English, has been published in 42 languages and has been a bestseller in all of them. Jostein Gaarder lives in Oslo with his family.

Jostein Gaarder

Sophie's World

What is Philosophy?
Dear Sophie,
Lots of people have hobbies. Some people collect old coins or foreign stamps, some do needlework, others spend most of their spare time on a particular sport.
A lot of people enjoy reading. But reading tastes differ widely. Some people only read newspapers or comics, some like reading **novels**, while others prefer books on astronomy, wildlife, or technological discoveries.
If I happen to be interested in horses or **precious stones**, I cannot expect everyone else to share my enthusiasm. If I watch all the sports programs on TV with great pleasure, I must put up with the fact that other people find sports boring.
Is there nothing that interests us all? Is there nothing that concerns everyone – no matter who they are or where they live in the world? Yes, dear Sophie, there are questions that certainly should interest everyone. They are precisely the questions this course is about.
What is the most important thing in life? If we ask someone living on the edge of **starvation**, the answer is food. If we ask someone dying of cold, the answer is warmth. If we put the same question to someone who feels lonely and isolated, the answer will probably be the company of other people.
But when these basic needs have been satisfied – will there still be something that everybody needs? Philosophers think so. They believe that man cannot live by bread alone. Of course everyone needs food. And everyone needs love and care. But there is something else – apart from that – which everyone needs, and that is to figure out who we are and why we are here.
Being interested in why we are here is not a 'casual' interest like collecting stamps. People who ask such questions are taking part in a debate that has gone on as long as man has lived on this planet. How the universe, the earth, and life came into being is a bigger and more important question than who won the most gold medals in the last Olympics.

Jostein Gaarder, Sophie's World, published in 1996 by Phoenix, London p. 11, 12

novel – a long, written story in which the characters and events are usually imaginary
precious stones – stones of great value, because of being very beautiful, rare or exclusive
starvation – suffering or death caused by lack of food

TIPP

Das Lesen von Texten dient nicht nur der Informationsentnahme. Es hilft Ihnen zudem bei der Erweiterung Ihres Wortschatzes und der Verbesserung Ihres Ausdrucksvermögens. Lesen Sie Originaltexte, auch wenn Sie nicht jedes Wort verstehen.

9 Read the following quotes taken from reviews.

'Sophie's World is set to become a unique popular classic: a wonderfully engaging mystery story that also forms a completely accessible and lucid introduction to philosophy and philosophers' (The Times)

'An extraordinary achievement' (Sunday Times)

'A terrifically entertaining and imaginative story wrapped round its tough, thought-provoking philosophical heart' (Independent on Sunday)

10 A lot of adjectives and adverbs are used in the reviews. Underline them. It is not necessary to understand them all.

TIPP

Adjektive bestimmen Nomen näher: *A* ***perfect*** *novel*
Adverbien bestimmen Verben und Adjektive: She can ***write*** **well**; oder: *a* **perfectly** *wrong decision*

11 The excerpt from Sophie's World (page 81) contains a lot of information. At the beginning you find ideas about how to spend your spare time. Make a word list on the topic "Spare Time".

....

....

12 The author expresses his ideas about basic needs and philosophical questions. Pick them out.

....

....

....

....

★ 13 What kind of text is it?

....

....

14 How old is the debate on why we are here?

....

....

Zwischentest

Martha K. Baker

In my country – directed by John Boorman

South Africa's Truth and Reconciliation Commission, (TRC) established in 1996, played an important role in that country's **transition** from apartheid to the current state of affairs, which is not a bit good. The TRC hearings which lasted two years gave more than 20,000 witnesses a chance to testify against their predominantly white **oppressors** in a courtroom. These hearings gave the world a demonstration of forgiveness and "ubuntu" (A South African word for **reconciliation**). The accused could attempt to explain their behaviour and could appeal for amnesty if they could prove that they were "just following orders", that their crimes were in fact politically motivated.

"In My Country" is a film based on the book by Afrikaans poet Antje Krog, a reporter who covered the **trials**. Ann Peacock wrote the screenplay from Krog's book, but in doing so, Peacock added sentimental drama where political drama would have been enough to make a serious movie.

The plot introduces two stars, who play roles that dominate the stories told during the trials of atrocities and terror attacks and just plain sadism. Anna Malan is a reporter, the daughter of Afrikaans farmers. Her father **decries** her work on the trials, her mother is more **conciliatory**, her husband is proud of her. When she joins the other reporters, she is met by her sound engineer, Dumi, who introduces her to an African-American reporter, Langston Whitfield. He comes with assumptions about his black skin. Her Dutch ancestry fights with his African roots. Despite their initial arguments, it is obvious that the two individuals are going to get together, over a beer if not in bed, for they are the main characters, played by the stars.

Juliette Binoche gives Anna a range of emotions from tearful and hysterical to shamed and guilty. Samuel L. Jackson plays Langston Whitfield with his **righteous** anger at the Afrikaans almost as fiery as his anger at his editor at the Washington Post for putting his stories on page seven instead of page one above the fold. **Pitting** their own personal animosities and assumptions, their Africanness versus their privileged status, means that tensions will **ride above the horizon like a haze**. But it also means that the viewer of *In My Country* hears the stories of the victims of apartheid through the filter of two lovers.

John Boorman directed In My Country with an eye toward the lovely, as in the sweeping aerial shots of Africa, as well as the ugly. Over his shots of skeletons, the words of the blacks, the mothers and widows, tell this story, one of thousands, before the commission. If you can peel away the glossy cover story to hear those stories more sharply, you can get the **kernel** of this time in South Africa's history. But you have to work at it.

---

http://kdhx.org/index.php?option=com_kdhxreview&task=details&id=1921&Itemid=263
KDHX Community Media, Saint Louis, Missouri. –

transition – change
reconciliation – healing, restored peace
decries – puts down
righteous – morally right
"ride above the horizon like a haze" – here: an image which means the tensions (their conflict) will always be present, hovering above them.
oppression – cruelty and injustice
trial – judicial examination in court with or without a jury
conciliatory – agreeable
pitting – matching against
kernel – centre

1 **Reading Comprehension – Decide whether the following statements are true** *T***, false** *F* **or not included in the review** *NI***.**

a) ___ The TRC was established during apartheid.

b) ___ Anna Malan's father approves of her job as a reporter.

c) ___ Langston Whitfield is African.

d) ___ The movie is meant for people interested in South African history.

e) ___ The mostly black South African victims of apartheid refused to testify at the trials.

f) ___ Those who committed atrocious crimes during apartheid could be set free if they proved that they were forced to do so.

g) ___ The two main characters have a love affair.

h) ___ L. Whitfield, played by Samuel Jackson, works for a British newspaper.

i) ___ Anna Malan plays a South African of Dutch origin.

j) ___ Filming took place in and around Cape Town and the Cape Peninsula.

k) ___ Antje Krog is the screenwriter of In My Country.

12 l) ___ During the trials Anna Malan feels sad about and ashamed of what happened in her country.

3 ★ **2** **Read the review again and write down three sentences or phrases which reveal the reviewer's opinion.**

3 **Language and vocabulary: Fill in the blanks with the correct form of the words in brackets.**

a) The African American reporter .... (assumption) that because Anna is white, she cannot understand the problems of black Africans.

b) Anna Malan shows great .... (proud) in her heritage.

c) Anna and Langston .... (argument) about the purpose of the TRC hearings.

d) The atmosphere during the trials is extremely .... (tension).

6 e) Anna was often overcome by .... (shamed) and .... (guilty).

21 **Gesamtpunktzahl**

Kontrollieren Sie Ihre Ergebnisse mithilfe der Lösungen (S. 122) und addieren Sie die erreichten Punkte.

☐ 21 bis 17 Punkte: ☺ ☐ 16 bis 11 Punkte: 😐 ☐ 10 bis 0 Punkte: ☹

Schreiben

Vorschau

→ Writing a summary or a comment
→ Creative writing
→ How to analyse a cartoon

Writing a summary

REGEL: Writing a summary

- Eine Zusammenfassung enthält das Wesentliche eines Textes.
- Sie gibt Antwort auf die fünf Fragen ***who, where, when, what, why.***
- Eine Zusammenfassung sollte im ***simple present*** und mit eigenen Worten verfasst werden.
- Sie enthält weder Beispiele noch andere Einzelheiten.
- In einer Zusammenfassung wird keine direkte Rede verwendet.
- Sie darf keine eigene Meinung oder Interpretation enthalten.

Vorgehensweise

- Lesen Sie den Text und schlagen Sie die unbekannten Wörter nach, die für das Textverständnis notwendig sind.
- Markieren Sie wichtige Aussagen, insbesondere die Stellen, die Antwort auf die Fragen **wer, wo, wann, was** und **warum** geben.
- Machen Sie sich Notizen zur Beantwortung der fünf Fragen.
- Achten Sie beim Schreiben der Zusammenfassung darauf, dass Sie durchgängig ***simple present*** verwenden, selbst wenn der Originaltext im ***past*** steht. Wechseln Sie auf keinen Fall zwischen ***present*** und ***past***.
- Sollte für die Zusammenfassung eine Wortzahl vorgegeben sein, müssen Sie diese einhalten und weder wesentlich mehr, noch weniger schreiben. Notfalls gehen Sie Ihre Zusammenfassung noch einmal durch und streichen Sie weniger wichtige Fakten. Auch durch die Sprache können Sie die Wortzahl verringern, z. B. durch den Gebrauch von Partizipien anstelle von Relativsätzen.
- Zum Schluss sollten Sie überprüfen, ob alle fünf Fragen beantwortet sind.
- Wenn Sie mit dem Inhalt Ihrer Zusammenfassung zufrieden sind, ist noch auf den Ausdruck und die sprachliche Richtigkeit zu achten.

TIPP

Gute Satzanfänge für ein Summary: The text/story may be divided in ... parts; The first part goes as far as line ... and deals with ...; In the second paragraph the author; The climax is reached when ...; In the last part ...

Lee Busselman

Locker 160

It was my idea, I guess, in the first place. “Let’s put a hate note in someone’s locker,” I said to Julie, half as a joke. We were waiting for biology class to begin. She smiled and raised her eyebrows. “Another one of your great ideas, Karen? Whose locker do you **suggest** we put it in?”

I glanced around the room. “Oh – Miriam.” It wasn’t that we really – I mean really – hated Miriam. That is, we both said “Good morning” to her and “See you tomorrow”. But she was just – well, different.

She was pretty, with long, black hair and a **graceful** figure, but she wasn’t popular. Miriam always kept to herself. Besides that, she wrote poetry, that **weird**, free verse kind that nobody can understand. That was how it began.

The next morning, Julie and I arrived at school early. We planned to write a note and put it in Miriam’s locker, number 160. “What should we say?” I asked. I held my pencil over a piece of notebook paper.

“Something simple. How about ‘You stink’?”

I printed the message in large, untidy letters. “There,” I said, handing the paper to Julie. “I don’t want it. You take it.” She pushed the note back. “I’m scared.” I didn’t want to, but I took the paper. My hands **trembled** as I walked down the hallway. I heard the loud clack of my footsteps on the linoleum. As I came near locker 160, I looked around to make sure nobody was watching. There was only Julie, peeking around the corner of the hall.

I opened Miriam’s locker. The books were neatly **piled** on a metal shelf. A notebook with ‘Miriam Laker’ written on it was beside them.

I placed our note on her notebook, where she would be sure to see it. I closed the locker door and walked away, with a pleasant feeling of **relief**. We stayed in the hall almost 15 minutes, waiting for Miriam to arrive. Then Julie **nudged** me and whispered, “Here she comes.”

Miriam went directly to the locker.

“Look,” Julie whispered. “Look at her face.”

We burst out laughing. It was clear that Miriam had seen the note. Her face looked as if she had been hit with a wet dish rag. Julie and I fled, **giggling**, to the rest room.

After that it was easy.

The next day, we arranged an open plastic bag of **marbles** in Miriam’s locker. When the hundreds of marbles went **bouncing** and **clattering** down the hallway, I wondered how she explained it to the principal. He was standing nearby when it happened.

After that, Julie got the idea of making a voodoo doll of Miriam. I must say we did an excellent job. We used a large carrot for the body, and a small onion with black yarn for the head.

After we drew the face on in **ink**, we stuck a huge hat pin through the onion. Then we hung a tiny sign on the doll that said ‘Miriam’. I thought it looked rather cute on the shelf of Miriam’s locker.

We reached a new height the next day. Julie had a **petition** to change the school dress code. It had been signed by almost our whole class, but it hadn’t been given to the principal yet. We copied all the names onto another sheet of paper, which said: “We, the undersigned, do **hereby** declare that Miriam Laker is weird, and do hereby announce that we hate her." Julie put the little gem in Miriam's locker, just before biology class. We waited in the biology room for Miriam to come in. We wanted to see how she had taken our last surprise. The bell rang, but Miriam still hadn't come.

"Maybe she isn't here today," Julie whispered to me. "She's never been late for a class before."

The period was almost over when we heard the **rescue squad** arrive at school. Our teacher left the room to find out what had happened. I could hear him talking to another teacher in the hall. "What's all this about?" our teacher asked.

"Oh, some girl – last name's Laker, I think – locked herself in the Home Ec room. She turned on the gas from all four stoves. They got her out just in time." "Did you hear that?" I asked Julie. She **nodded** in **amazement**. "Well," I whispered, "I always knew that anyone who wrote poetry would come to a bad end."

We began to laugh.

---

suggest – tell someone your ideas about what they should do
graceful – having an attractive shape or form
weird – very strange and unusual, and difficult to understand
tremble – shake slightly in a way that you cannot control, especially because you are upset or frightened
pile – fill a place or contain
relief – a feeling of comfort when something frightening, worrying, or painful has ended or has not happened
nudge – push someone gently, usually with your elbow, in order to get their attention
giggle – laugh quickly, quietly, and in a high voice, because something is funny or because you are nervous or embarrassed
marble – a small coloured glass ball that children roll along the ground as part of a game
bounce – if a ball or other object bounces, or you bounce it, it immediately moves up or away from a surface after hitting it
clatter – if heavy hard objects clatter, or if you clatter them, they make a loud unpleasant noise
ink – a coloured liquid that you use for writing, printing or drawing
petition – a written request signed by a lot of people, asking someone in authority to do something or change something
hereby – as a result of this statement
rescue squad – ambulance
nod – move your head up and down, especially in order to show agreement or understanding
amazement – a feeling of great surprise

★ **1 Write a summary of "Locker 160" in about 100 words. First of all answer briefly the five WH-questions (where, when, who, what, why) in order to structure your summary.**

TIPP

Die englische Entsprechung für „die Geschichte spielt" ist ***the story is set (in)***;
für „die Handlung spielt":
the action takes places (in).

Creative writing

REGEL: A missing part of a story or an ending

- Grundlegende Voraussetzung für das Schreiben eines fehlenden Abschnitts, eines Texts oder eines Endes ist das sichere Textverständnis.
- Der zu verfassende Teil muss sich sowohl logisch aus der Textvorlage ergeben als auch kreative Elemente enthalten.
- Er darf nicht im Widerspruch zu Aussagen im Text oder zu Charaktereigenschaften stehen, die sich aus dem Text ableiten lassen.
- Daher ist es notwendig, sowohl die beschriebene Situation als auch die Figuren zu verstehen und sich mit ihnen zu identifizieren. Nur so ist eine überzeugende Ergänzung der Textvorlage möglich.
- Überzeugend ist es, inhaltliche Elemente der Textvorlage zu verarbeiten.
- Neben inhaltlichen Aspekten ist die Sprache sehr wichtig, die sich möglichst wenig von der des Originaltextes unterscheiden sollte.

Toeckey Jones was born and grew up in South Africa, but in 1971 moved to London where he now lives and works as a full-time writer. His first novel, "Go Well, Stay Well", was published in 1979, and was welcomed as one of the few novels for young readers to describe what it is like to grow up in a ***racially segregated society.***

Toeckey Jones

The Meeting (1979)

Candice is a 17-year-old white South African girl from Johannesburg. One day, while walking in the city, she **trips** and **twists her ankle.**

Almost immediately she felt a gentle touch on her arm. She opened her eyes to see a young African girl standing in front of her. Instinctively, Candy's **grip** on her bag tightened. The girl could be after her money. Candy knew how clever the young black pickpockets in the city were said to be. She was always being warned to keep a close hold on her purse.

"You OK?" Without waiting for an answer, the girl bent down to inspect Candy's ankle.

"Tch ... tch ... shame." Shaking her head she straightened up.

"That's no good to walk on," she said. "You can sit down in the park. It's not far. Come, I must help you."

The girl took hold of Candy's free arm and after a moment's **hesitation**, Candy allowed herself to be supported as they began to move slowly along the pavement.

"Too many drinks, hey?" the girl **teased**.

Candy laughed, then felt herself **blushing** as she became aware of the curious stares they were attracting. She tried to move faster, leaning as little as possible on the supporting arm beside her. She still wasn't sure she could trust the girl. It would have been so much

simpler if it had been a white person who had offered help. She didn't know why the girl was doing it. Should she offer to pay her? It was all rather **embarrassing**.
The park was only two blocks away, but it seemed an age before they got there. As the girl helped her down into a sitting position on the grass, Candy was aware of her bag slipping off her shoulder and the girl stretching out to catch it as it fell. Candy held her breath, her heart beating fast. But the girl didn't run off. Instead, she waited until Candy was sitting comfortably, and then handed the bag to her.
"Better now?" she asked.
While the girl bent down to take a closer look at the **injured** ankle, Candy studied her thoughtfully. She was really rather pretty, Candy discovered to her surprise, for she had never thought of African features as being attractive before. But this girl's features were all in perfect proportion to each other giving her face as a whole an open, sunny expression.
Candy didn't want her to go. She had never met an African girl of her own age before – at least not to speak to. And she was already beginning to like this girl who seemed undecided about her next move and was playing nervously with the **worn collar** of her blouse, trying to do up a button that wasn't there.
"Are you in hurry?" Candy asked.
"No, Why? Can I give you a lift home? My Mercedes is just round the corner."
Candy laughed and the girl sat down on the grass beside her.
"What's your name?" she asked.
"Candice. But everyone calls me Candy. And yours?"
"Rebecca. But everyone calls me Becky." And then they both laughed. "Tell you what." Candy said. "I'm thirsty. How about you?"
"Sure. What would you like? I'll go and get it. Beer?"
"I think I'd better have a Coke. But let's go and sit down somewhere, and perhaps have something to eat as well. So long as I don't have to walk too far, my ankle should be all right."
"You know a place we can go?" Becky asked.
Candy's face slowly **reddened** with embarrassment. For a moment she had completely forgotten. There wasn't anywhere they could go together. Within ten minutes' walk of where they were sitting, there were at least three restaurants or coffee bars. But Becky couldn't go into them – they were all **exclusively** for whites. Further away there were a few cafés for African workers travelling daily into Johannesburg from the black township of Soweto. But even if Candy could have walked that far with her bad ankle, she would be stopped from going into any of them with Becky.
"Do you want us to get **arrested**?" Becky teased.

The two girls continue to talk for some time and agree to meet again. Candy then telephones her father and asks him to come and fetch her.

Candy caught sight of a blue Cortina and identified her father at the wheel.
"My dad's here," she said unnecessarily, for Becky had already got to her feet and was quickly brushing the grass off her skirt.
"I must go," she told Candy.

"Wait ... Hold on, we haven't **settled** anything. We don't even know how to get in touch with each other."

Candy wasn't really surprised that Becky wanted to get away before her father arrived, but she wanted the two of them to meet. It would make it easier to talk about Becky to her father later.

Suddenly Candy's father came up behind them.

"What have you done to yourself?" he called out to Candy. Becky turned round and immediately stepped aside, separating herself from the other two.

"Hello, Dad," Candy said. "Dad, this is Becky," she went on quickly. "She's been helping me and looking after me."

"Oh." He turned and glanced at Becky, who **bowed** her head shyly.

"Good afternoon, sir," she said politely.

"Uh ... hello." He was already bending down to look at Candy's ankle.

"Is it very painful?" he asked.

Candy shook her head impatiently. She was aware that Becky had moved a little further away and was **fidgeting** nervously.

"Dad!" Candy said firmly. "Becky has been absolutely **marvellous**. I don't know what I would have done without her."

"Oh." He smiled briefly in Becky's direction. "That was very kind of her. Now, do you think you'll be able to walk as far as the car?"

Candy was disappointed. He could at least show some interest in Becky, and talk to her directly. She pulled a face at him, and **glanced** at Becky.

"What?... Oh, yes, of course."

Too late. Candy realised that he had misunderstood her. Putting his hand into his pocket, he said,

"Here, this is for being so kind and looking after my daughter until I got here," and he held a one **rand** note out to her.

Helplessly, Candy stared at them both, red with shame. Anything she said now could only make the situation worse. She felt **furious** with her father, but she knew she couldn't really **blame** him for misunderstanding her. One glance at Becky was enough to see how poor she was. And normally white people automatically **tipped** Africans for any help they gave. But after everything that had passed between her and Becky, offering Becky money could only seem an **insult**.

Candy couldn't **bear** to watch but she had to. She saw Becky look up and slowly begin to shake her head.

Toeckey Jones: "The Meeting", from Go Well, Stay Well, © The Bodley Head, London 1979; in: Step up, Diesterweg 1991

racially segregated society – a society in which people of different races are kept apart so that they live, work, or study separately
trip – hit something with your foot by accident so that you fall or almost fall
twists one's ankle – hurt your ankle (the joint between your foot and your leg) by pulling or turning it too suddenly while you are moving
grip – the way you hold something tightly
hesitation – a pause before doing something especially when you are nervous, embarrassed, or worried
tease – make jokes in order to have fun by embarrassing someone, here in a friendly way
blush – become red in the face, usually because you are embarrassed
embarrassing – making you feel ashamed, nervous, or uncomfortable
injured – having a wound or damage to part of your body
worn – old and damaged, especially because it has been used a lot

collar – the part of a shirt, coat etc that fits around your neck, and is usually folded over
redden – become red
exclusively – only
arrest – if the police arrest someone, the person is taken to a police station because the police think they have done something illegal
settle – decide what you are going to do, especially so that you can make definite arrangements
bow – bend the top part of your body forward in order to show respect for someone important
fidget – keep moving your hands or feet, especially because you are nervous
marvellous – wonderful
rand – the standard unit of money in South Africa
furious – very angry
blame – responsibility for a mistake or for something bad
glance – a quick look
tip – give an additional amount of money to someone
insult – a remark or action that is offensive or deliberately rude
bear – stand, endure

2 **Write a summary of the story "The Meeting" in 100–150 words.**

★ **3** **The story "The Meeting" (pp. 88–90) has an open ending. Continue the story in about 150 words.**

REGEL: Writing a dialogue

- Beachten Sie die richtige Wiedergabe der direkten Rede, im Englischen sind die Anführungszeichen immer oben ("...").
- Im Englischen steht ein Komma (statt Doppelpunkt) zwischen dem Satz, der die Rede einleitet, und der wörtlichen Rede.
- Gesprochenes ist oft weniger formell als Geschriebenes. Je nach Sprecher und Anlass ist also auch Umgangssprache möglich.
- Sie müssen einen geeigneten Anfang und ein passendes Ende des Gesprächs finden.
- Auch hier ist es äußerst wichtig, sich mit den Personen zu identifizieren (Alter, Charakter, Herkunft, daraus resultierende Sprache, Haltung).
- Manchmal ist es ratsam, eine Einführung zur Erläuterung der Situation zu schreiben, die aber kurz gehalten werden sollte.

★ **4** **Write a dialogue between Candy and her father after leaving Becky behind in about 300 words ("The Meeting", pp. 88–90).**

Comment writing

REGEL: Writing a comment

- Unter ***comment*** versteht man eine schriftliche begründete Stellungnahme zu einem Thema, einer Aussage, einer Frage oder einem Cartoon.
- Die Stellungnahme besteht aus drei grundsätzlichen Teilen: ***introduction*** (Einleitung), ***main part*** (Hauptteil), ***conclusion*** (Schlussfolgerung).
- In der Einleitung wird die zur Diskussion stehende Aussage mit eigenen Worten wiedergegeben.
- Im Hauptteil werden die Argumente und Gründe zum Thema erläutert.
  Wichtig: **Argument + Beleg/Erklärung + Beispiel**! Keine bloße Aneinanderreihung von Argumenten!
- Achten Sie auf sinnvolle Verknüpfungen (siehe ***Useful phrases,*** Seite 93/94).
- Struktur der Argumente: vom weniger Wichtigen zum Wichtigen
- Der Schluss fasst die gesamte Argumentation noch einmal in einem wertenden Urteil zusammen; hier können Sie Ihre eigene Meinung (Zustimmung/Ablehnung) einbringen.

TIPP

Allgemeine Hinweise zum Schreiben

- Lesen Sie die Aufgabenstellung zum Schreiben immer genau (wenn notwendig auch mehrmals) durch und achten Sie auf die geforderte Umsetzung.
- Wählen Sie eine Stilebene, die der Aufgabenstellung angemessen ist.
- Überlegen Sie, welche Zeitform Sie verwenden müssen. Häufig geht dies aus der Fragestellung oder der Art der Aufgabe hervor.
- Wechseln Sie nicht zwischen verschiedenen Varianten des Englischen, entscheiden Sie sich entweder für das britische oder das amerikanische Englisch.
- Beginnen Sie die Umsetzung der Aufgabenstellung mit einer Mindmap oder einer Stichwortsammlung, in denen Sie Ideen für Ihren Text sammeln und sortieren, bevor Sie mit dem eigentlichen Schreiben des Textes beginnen.
- Gliedern Sie Ihren Text in Sinneinheiten.
- Nehmen Sie immer ausreichend Zeit zum Kontrolllesen und für die Korrektur. Das schließt auch ein, dass Sie überprüfen, ob Sie die Aufgabenstellung vollständig und richtig erfüllt haben.

★ **5** **Comment on the following statement: "All people are equal, no matter who they are or where they come from." (300 – 450 words)**

Useful phrases and expressions for writing

1) Einleitung

As we know ...	Wie wir wissen, ...
It is often claimed / said / stated that ...	Es wird oft behauptet / gesagt, ...
It is commonly / generally believed that ...	Allgemein glaubt man, ...
It goes without saying ...	Es versteht sich von selbst, ...

2) Hauptteil – Argumentation

Meinungsäußerung

I would say ...	Ich würde sagen, ...
I am convinced that ...	Ich bin überzeugt (davon), dass ...
I personally believe / think that ...	Ich persönlich denke / glaube, dass ...
In my opinion / from my point of view ...	Meiner Meinung nach ...
It seems to me that ...	Es scheint mir, dass ...

Aufzählung

Firstly ... secondly ... thirdly	Erstens ... zweitens ... drittens
On the one hand ... on the other hand	Einerseits ... andererseits
First of all ... then ... finally ...	Zuallererst ... dann ... schließlich / zum Schluss ...
To begin / start with ...	Zuerst
The first (second, next, last) point I'd like to mention / make is ...	Den ersten (zweiten, nächsten, letzten) Punkt, den ich nennen möchte, ...
First and foremost ...	Zuallererst ...
Last but not least ...	Nicht zuletzt / nicht zu vergessen ...

Beispiele

For example / instance ...	Zum Beispiel ...
Let me give you a couple of examples ...	Lasst mich ein paar Beispiele nennen / anführen ...
Take for example ...	Nimm zum Beispiel ...
You only have to think of / Just think of ...	Du brauchst nur mal an ... zu denken / Denk mal an ...

Ergänzungen

Furthermore / besides / in addition to this ...	Außerdem ...
Moreover ...	Überdies, ferner ...
Another / a further point ...	Ein weiterer Punkt ...
Apart from ...	Abgesehen von ...
It must also be said that ...	Man muss auch sagen, dass ...
In general / on the whole / generally speaking ...	Im Allgemeinen ...
As a rule ...	Normalerweise ...
I want to highlight / stress / emphasise ...	Ich möchte betonen / hervorheben, ...
It is important / vital to realise that ...	Es ist wichtig / unerlässlich zu erkennen, dass ...
It is certainly true that ...	Es ist sicherlich richtig, dass ...
It is (very) clear / certain that ...	Es ist (sehr) offensichtlich / klar / sicher, dass ...
... as everyone knows.	... wie jederman weiß.
It is difficult to believe that ...	Es fällt einem schwer zu glauben, dass ...
... seems possible / likely / unlikely.	... scheint möglich / wahrscheinlich / unwahrscheinlich ...
In other words/To put it in another way ...	Mit anderen Worten / Anders gesagt ...

Gegenargumente und Einschränkungen

However ...	Jedoch ...
Although ...	Obwohl ...
There is no denying that ...	Es lässt sich nicht bestreiten, dass ...
On the contrary / In contrast / By comparison with ...	Im Gegenteil / Im Gegensatz / Verglichen mit ...
Whereas ...	Wohingegen / während ...
Despite / In spite of ...	Trotz ...
Nevertheless ...	Trotzdem / dennoch ...

3) Zusammenfassung

In short / Thus / Therefore ...	Kurz gesagt / Folglich / Deshalb ...
To summarise / sum up / conclude / All in all ...	Zusammenfassend / abschließend / Insgesamt ...
Having considered all these issues ...	Nachdem ich all diese Punkte betrachtet habe, ...

How to analyse a cartoon

Ein Cartoon (Karikatur) ist eine komisch überzeichnende Darstellung einer Situation in einem Bild, die oft kritische oder komische Züge trägt und häufig in Tageszeitungen/Zeitschriften erscheint.

Definition of the noun "cartoon" in English:

> **1** – A simple drawing showing the features of its subjects in a humorously exaggerated way, especially a satirical one in a newspaper or magazine: *the minister faced a welter of hostile headlines and mocking cartoons*
>
> **1.1** – (also **cartoon strip**) A narrative sequence of humorous drawings in a comic, magazine, or newspaper, usually with captions: *a Peanuts cartoon by Charles Schulz*
>
> **1.2** – A simplified or exaggerated version or interpretation of something: [as modifier]: *Dolores becomes a cartoon housewife, reading glossy magazines in a bathrobe*
>
> **2** – A film using animation techniques to photograph a sequence of drawings rather than real people or objects: *we watched Yogi Bear cartoons on TV*
>
> **3** – A full-size drawing made by an artist as a preliminary design for a painting or other work of art: *the tapestries are based on a set of cartoons commissioned by Pope Leo XI*
>
> www.oxforddictionaries.com/definition/english/cartoon

Wenn man einen Cartoon bearbeiten soll, gibt es zwei Schwerpunkte, auf die man sich konzentrieren muss: die Beschreibung *(description)* und die Analyse *(analysis)*.

REGEL: Zur **Beschreibung** gehören:

- Ort/Handlung
- Objekte und Personen
- Symbole
- Sprechblasen
- Überschriften/Bildunterschriften/Beschriftungen/Anmerkungen/Zahlen/Daten ...
- Geräusche (BANG! ROOAR, Zzzzz ...)

Beschreiben Sie nur die Elemente, die für die Analyse und das Verständnis des Cartoons wichtig sind. Hier ist noch keine Interpretation oder eigene Meinung gefragt.

Die **Analyse** beinhaltet:

- Kernaussage des Cartoons
- Intention des Zeichners
- Zwischen den Zeilen lesen: Bezug nehmen auf das aktuelle Geschehen/historische Hintergründe/gesellschaftliche Konventionen/politische Ereignisse ...

Bei der Analyse nehmen Sie Bezug auf Symbole, Beschriftungen, Objekte usw. aus der Beschreibung und integrieren sie in Ihre Interpretation. Hier dürfen Sie auch Ihre eigene Meinung darlegen. Erklären Sie außerdem die Stimmung, Körpersprache, Gesichtsausdrücke, Anordnung von Objekten zueinander und die Wirkung auf den Leser.

http://nieonline.com/cftc/pdfs/newspapersfuture.pdf

6 Describe the cartoon by Mike Keefe.

a) Where does the action take place?

....

....

....

b) Make a list of the people / objects in the cartoon.

....

....

....

....

c) Which objects are symbols? What for?

....

....

....

....

d) Describe the action including the text in the speech balloons.
(Use your own words.)

....

....

....

....

....

....

7 Answer the questions as a guideline for an analysis.

a) How do the speech balloons support the symbols?

....

....

....

b) What do the people in the cartoon stand for?

....

....

....

....

c) Explain the message conveyed by the cartoon.

....

....

....

....

★ d) Between the lines:
Which is the current situation of newspapers because of New Media tools?

....

....

....

....

....

....

Wortschatztafel Cartoon

*no **pure** description*	keine **reine** Beschreibung
*In my opinion the cartoon **is supposed to** ...*	Meiner Meinung nach **soll** die Karikatur ...
*to **make fun of / poke** fun at a politician*	**sich über** einen Politiker **lustig machen**
*to strongly **criticize** his policy*	seine Politik scharf **kritisieren**
*to **satirize** human stupidity*	menschliche Dummheit **satirisch darstellen**
*to **ridicule** silly behaviour*	dummes Verhalten **lächerlich machen**
*to **mock** a trend*	einen Trend **verspotten**
*to **condemn** hypocrisy*	Heuchelei **verurteilen**
*The cartoonist may want to **convey** that ...*	Der Karikaturist will vielleicht **vermitteln**, dass ...
*His **message** might be that ...*	Seine **Botschaft** könnte sein, dass ...
*His **point** seems to be that ...*	**Er will** offensichtlich **darauf hinaus**, dass ...
*Perhaps his **intention** is to show that ...*	Vielleicht ist es seine **Absicht** zu zeigen, dass ...
*You can **tell** she's stupid **by the way** she talks.*	Man kann **an** ihrer Sprechweise **sehen**, dass ...
*Her stupidity **comes out** in her speech.*	Ihre Dummheit **zeigt sich** in ihrer Ausdrucksweise.
*His body language **reveals** that ...*	Seine Körpersprache **zeigt**, dass ...
*You **see from** his facial expression, that ...*	Man **sieht an** seinem Gesichtsausdruck, dass ...
*The ... **stands for / symbolizes** ...*	Der ... **steht für / symbolisiert** ...
*The ... is a **symbol of** ...*	Der ... ist ein **Symbol für** ...
*His gesture **implies** that ...*	Seine Geste **deutet daraufhin / impliziert**, dass ...
*His clothes **correspond to** ...*	Seine Kleidung **entspricht** ...
*a **satirical** drawing*	eine **satirische** Zeichnung
*to **refer to** ...*	**sich beziehen auf ...**
*a hidden **reference to** the past*	ein versteckter **Hinweis auf** die Vergangenheit
*to **allude to** a current event*	**auf** ein aktuelles Ereignis **anspielen**
*a witty **allusion to** a film*	eine geistreiche **Anspielung auf** einen Film
*a **speech bubble** (thought bubble)*	eine Sprechblase (Gedankenblase)
*a funny **caption***	eine komische **Bildunterschrift**
*At **first glance** one might think that ...*	Auf den **ersten Blick** könnte man meinen, dass ...
*A closer **analysis**, however, shows that ...*	Eine genauere **Analyse** zeigt jedoch, dass ...
*On a **superficial** level one might think ...*	**Oberflächlich** betrachtet könnte man meinen ...
*On the **figurative** level ...*	Auf der **übertragenen** Ebene ...
*You could **draw the conclusion** that ...*	Man könnte **den Schluss ziehen**, dass ...
*to **exaggerate** character traits*	Charaktereigenschaften **übertreiben**
*a **slight** exaggeration*	eine **leichte** Übertreibung
*a **gross** exaggeration*	eine **grobe** Übertreibung
*a **distorted** image of ...*	ein **verzerrtes** Bild von ...
*to **contribute to** the message*	**zu** der Botschaft **beitragen**

Zwischentest

★ 1 **Describe and analyse the cartoon.**
You can use the word list for cartoons on page 98 to spice up your language.

Gesamtpunktzahl: 20

Kontrollieren Sie Ihre Ergebnisse mithilfe der Lösungen (S. 124) und addieren Sie die erreichten Punkte.

☐ 20 bis 16 Punkte: ☺ ☐ 15 bis 10 Punkte: 😐 ☐ 9 bis 0 Punkte: ☹

Mediation/Sprachmittlung

Vorschau

→ Wodurch unterscheidet sich die Mediation von der Übersetzung?
→ Wann ist eine Mediation eine gute Sprachmittlung?

Mediation sorgt für „Verstehen"

REGEL: Ziel der Mediation ist es, einem Gesprächspartner mit geringen oder fehlenden Fremdsprachenkenntnissen wichtige Informationen aus einem Text oder einer Aussage zu vermitteln. Dies bedeutet nicht, einen Text wortwörtlich wiederzugeben, sondern den Inhalt verständlich in eine andere Sprache zu übertragen. Im Gegensatz zur traditionellen Übersetzung ist es hierbei u. a. möglich/notwendig, schwierige Wörter und Satzstrukturen zu umschreiben, eine angemessene Sprachebene zu wählen und gegebenenfalls kulturelle bzw. inhaltliche Besonderheiten zu erläutern.

TIPP

- **Für wen** machen Sie die Sprachmittlung (Freund, Firmenchef, Gastfamilie, etc.)? Je nach Adressat müssen Sie auf Wortwahl, Ausdrucksweise und Sprachebene (formal, umgangssprachlich, etc.) achten.
- Welche Gesichtspunkte werden in der **Aufgabenstellung** verlangt? Je nach Aufgabenstellung müssen Sie eine vollständige Zusammenfassung eines Textes schreiben oder nur Teilaspekte herausarbeiten.
- Wie gehe ich mit **schwierigen Wörtern und Strukturen** um? Umschreiben Sie unbekannte Ausdrücke und verwenden Sie typische Strukturen der jeweiligen Zielsprache.
- Was mache ich mit **kulturspezifischen Begriffen**? Sie werden nicht übersetzt, müssen aber näher erläutert werden, auch wenn die Erklärung nicht im Original enthalten ist.

Jugendherbergen – günstig übernachten

Ob Klassenfahrten, Ausflüge mit einem Verein oder private Reisen – fast jeder Jugendliche in Deutschland hat schon einmal in einer Jugendherberge übernachtet.
Die Idee, günstige Unterkünfte für junge Menschen einzurichten, hatte der deutsche Lehrer Richard Schirrmann (1874–1961). Auf einer Wanderung wurden er und seine Schüler von einem Gewitter überrascht. Da es keine andere Unterkunft gab, übernachteten sie in einer Dorfschule.
Nach diesem Erlebnis dachte sich Schirrmann, dass es überall Unterkünfte für junge Wanderer geben sollte. Im Jahr 1912 eröffnete er dann die erste Jugendherberge und ein Jahr später einen Verband der Jugendherbergen, der heute Deutsches Jugendherbergswerk (DJH) heißt.
Wer günstig in einer deutschen Jugendherberge übernachten will, muss Mitglied im DJH sein. Die Mitglieder zahlen einen jährlichen Beitrag und bekommen eine Mitgliedskarte. Mit dieser Karte können sie in deutschen Jugendherbergen übernachten, die zwar hauptsächlich von jungen Menschen besucht werden, aber auch immer mehr ältere Gäste beherbergen. Diese zahlen dann mehr pro Übernachtung.
Jugendherbergen unterscheiden sich von anderen kommerziellen Unterkünften wie Hotels und Pensionen darin, dass sie zum Beispiel Gemeinschaftsräume haben, damit sich die jungen Leute kennenlernen und gemeinsame Aktivitäten planen können. Wer also in einer deutschen Jugendherberge übernachtet, lernt nicht nur junge Leute aus der ganzen Welt kennen, sondern kann auch sein Wissen über Deutschland erweitern.

gekürzt aus: www.pasch-net.de/pas/cls/leh/unt/dst/mob/de3361227.htm

★ **1** **Erzähle deinem Freund Jay aus America, wie die Idee zu Jugendherbergen in Deutschland entstanden ist, was man braucht, um an einer Jugendherberge zu übernachten, wo die Unterschiede zu etwa einem Hotel liegen und was die Vorteile dieser Art der Unterkünfte sind.**

2 **The travel tips about Eisenach and Cuxhaven describe famous personalities and landmarks. Explain to an English-speaking tourist what these cities offer. Be aware to give short extra information where necessary.**

Eisenach – Geschichte zum Anfassen

Die Stadt Eisenach (Thüringen) hat doppelte historische Bedeutung.
Der Eisenacher Johann Sebastian Bach hat dort seine Musik komponiert. Und Martin Luther hat sich auf der Wartburg bei Eisenach versteckt. Touristen können in der Wartburg den Raum besichtigen, in dem Luther die Bibel in die deutsche Sprache übersetzt hat. Schön ist der Blick vom Burgturm auf den Ort. Von dort sieht man auch das Bachhaus. Das Museum zeigt die Arbeit und das Leben von Johann Sebastian Bach.

Deutsch Perfekt 3/2009, S. 63

Cuxhaven – ruhige Strände

Nicht nur im Sommer ist die Nordseeküste eine schöne Region für den Urlaub.
Im Frühling ist es an den langen Stränden noch ganz ruhig. Das ist die ideale Zeit für Wanderungen durch das Watt. Zum Beispiel vor Cuxhaven (Niedersachsen). Dort gibt es zu jeder Zeit Wanderungen zu verschiedenen Themen. Zum Beispiel kann man dabei etwas über die Tiere im Watt oder über Bernstein erfahren.

Deutsch Perfekt 3/2009, S. 63

Zwischentest

Olympia: Kati Wilhelm ist schon ganz aufgeregt

Munio/Leichlingen (RPO). **Die dreimalige Biathlon-Olympiasiegerin Kati Wilhelm bereitet sich mit der deutschen Mannschaft derzeit im finnischen Munio auf die Olympia-Saison vor. Sie stand Schülern Rede und Antwort.**

Michael: Welche Sportarten finden Sie bei den Olympischen Spielen am besten?

Kati Wilhelm: Natürlich Biathlon, das ist ja auch besonders spannend. Aber ich mag fast jede Sportart. Bei den Sommerspielen interessiere ich mich vor allem für Leichtathletik und Schwimmen. Im Winter schaue ich auch Langlauf und Skispringen, aber da habe ich nicht so viel Zeit, weil ich ja selbst zu Wettkämpfen muss.

Vanessa: Dopen Sie?

Kati Wilhelm: Nein, natürlich nicht, ich verabscheue das. Es gibt immer wieder Fälle, zum Glück noch nicht in unserer Mannschaft. Wir sind absolut dagegen. Und wir setzen uns für scharfe Kontrollen ein.

Tobias: Wie viel Geld verdienen Sie?

Kati Wilhelm: Das ist eine gute Frage. Beim Weltcup gibt es bestimmte Prämien. Für einen Sieg 10 000 Euro brutto, das sind nach Abzug der Steuern und Abgaben in Deutschland ungefähr noch 5000 Euro. Für Platz acht aber gibt es nur noch 500 Euro. Bei Weltmeisterschaften und Olympischen Spielen liegen die Prämien höher. Hinzu kommen Sponsorengelder, die Höhe richtet sich auch nach dem Erfolg.

Jonathan: Sind Sie vor den Olympischen Spielen sehr aufgeregt?

Kati Wilhelm: Ich glaube schon. Olympische Spiele sind ja ganz etwas Besonderes, weil sie nur alle vier Jahre stattfinden. Es gehört einfach dazu, dass man aufgeregt ist. Es ist ja auch wichtig, dass einem nicht alles am ... vorbeigeht.

Franziska: Haben Sie berühmte Freunde?

Kati Wilhelm: Die meisten aus unserer Mannschaft sind ja recht berühmt. Aber mit berühmten Menschen aus anderen Richtungen bin ich nicht befreundet. Wenn man den Klitschkos mal die Hand schüttelt, ist man ja mit denen nicht gleich befreundet.

Nathalie: Wie gehen Sie mit Ihren Erfolgen um?

Zwischentest

Kati Wilhelm: Ich kann damit, glaube ich, ganz gut umgehen. Meine Familie und meine Freunde helfen mir auch, auf dem Boden zu bleiben. Ich bin sicher stolz auf meine Erfolge, gehe aber gelassen damit um. Das funktioniert ganz gut.
Julian: Rauchen Sie?
Kati Wilhelm: Nein, das wäre ja nicht gut für mich. Genauso wie es für alle Menschen ungesund ist. In unserer Sportart brauchen wir besonders ein großes Lungenvolumen. Wenn ich rauchen würde, könnte ich das Training gleich drangeben, dann würde es keinen Sinn mehr machen.

Adapted interview (http://www.rp-online.de/sport/olympia/winter/projekt/Olympia-Kati-Wilhelm-ist-schon-ganz-aufgeregt_aid_785728.html)

★ 1 **You're on an exchange program in Vancouver/Canada. Your teacher asks you to write an article about a German athlete for the "Olympic section 2010" in the school magazine. Fortunately, Kati Wilhelm, a famous German biathlete, gave an interview at your school two days before you left. Write an article about Kati Wilhelm for the magazine using the information from the interview.**

35 **Gesamtpunktzahl**

Kontrollieren Sie Ihre Ergebnisse mithilfe der Lösungen (S. 125) und addieren Sie die erreichten Punkte.
☐ 35 bis 28 Punkte: ☺ ☐ 27 bis 18 Punkte: 😐 ☐ 17 bis 0 Punkte: 😕

Abschlusstest

In his book 'Caught in the Crossfire', Alan Gibbons tells the story of a British-Asian family. Diane Khan, a white Englishwoman, has been married for seventeen years to Suhail, a British Asian whose parents originally came from Pakistan. They live in Oakfield with their two teenage children, Rabia and Tahir.

Alan Gibbons

Caught in the Crossfire

Rabia walks into the kitchen and finds her mother staring out at the little **back yard** smiling to herself.

"What are you smiling at?" she asks, already smiling herself. They are about as close as mother and daughter can be. One smiles and the other smiles with her. One cries and they end up **weeping** together.

"I was just thinking about Tahir," Diane explains. "Do you remember what he was like when he first started **fasting**?"

Rabi laughs. "Do I? He was so **miserable**."

"I know," says Diane. "He wasn't a very good Muslim at that time, was he?"

She allows the smile to **fade** slowly. Her son is a good Muslim now, and getting better every day. In fact, it is Tahir who **pushes** Suhail to go along to the **mosque**. For some reason, though she hates herself for thinking it, that scares Diane. Her son is growing into a proud, **single-minded** individual. Carry your head as high as Tahir does and somebody **is bound to** want to **knock it off**.

"He's so different these days," she says, remembering the loving, impulsive boy he was. "Such a serious young man."

It's true. Over the **last couple of years** he has taken his **obligations** seriously. He never complains. When he fasts for Ramadan he does so with astonishing self-control for somebody who loves his food so much. As he has grown into a young man he has shown greater and greater pride in his Pakistani **ancestry**. **Painfully aware** that Oakfield's communities are pulling apart, he seems to be drawing his Muslim identity around him as a protective **cloak**. That other part of him, the part she gave him, seems to be **shrinking** by the day. Diane sometimes wonders if she hasn't become something of an embarrassment to him.

"Tahir's all right," says Rabia. "Just a bit earnest, that's all."

"That's **a nice way of putting it**," says Diane, **winking**. "Now say what you really mean."

Rabia grins. "OK then, **pompous**. You know that new top I bought?"

"For Sofia's birthday party?"

Rabia nods. "Do you know what he said to me?"

Diane shakes her head.

"Only that I was showing too much."

"Never!"

Rabia **nods**. "He did. He meant it too. He thinks I'm **immodest**."

Diane shakes her head.

"He's just getting that from his friends. Honestly, you'd think he never looked at a girl. Remember last summer."

"The girl on the beach?"

"Yes, the one in the bikini. It was lust at first sight. His eyes were out on stalks. He didn't think she was showing too much."

Tahir walks in at that very moment. He is wearing that studied, serious expression he has been perfecting. Rabia and Diane immediately burst out laughing.

"What's the matter with you two?" he demands.

"Oh, nothing."

He gives them both a suspicious look, then adds: "When do we eat?"

That only sets them off again. They laugh until they have forgotten why they ever started.

Alan Gibbons, Orion Children's, 2003

back yard – area at the back of a house
weeping – crying
fasting – not eating for a certain time
miserable – very unhappy
fade – slowly disappear
push – here: encourage
mosque – building in which Muslims worship
single-minded – person with a strong will
is bound to – is likely to
knock it off – here: bring s.o. down to earth
last couple of years – last few years
obligations – things you have to do
ancestry – family and cultural roots
painfully aware – not liking sth. but noticing it is true
cloak – coat
shrinking – getting smaller
a nice way of putting it – here: making it sound better than it is
winking – quickly closing and opening one eye as a sign to s.o.
pompous – behaving as if you are very important
nod – moving your head to show you agree
immodest – here: indecent

A Sprachliche Mittel

1 Tenses: Say what tenses are used in these sentences and why.

a) "What are you smiling at?" she asks. (line 3)
b) "I was just thinking about Tahir," Diane explains. (line 6)
c) "He wasn't a very good Muslim at that time, was he?" (line 9)
d) In fact, it is Tahir who pushes Suhail to go along to the mosque. (line 11)
e) Over the last couple of years he has taken his obligations seriously. (line 17)
14 f) He is wearing that studied, serious expression he has been perfecting (line 39/40).

★ **2 Reported Speech: Rewrite the following paragraphs using reported speech. Start like this: Diane explained ...**

a) "I was just thinking about Tahir," Diane explains. "Do you remember what he was like when he first started fasting?"
Rabi laughs. "... He was so miserable."
"I know," says Diane. "He wasn't a very good Muslim at that time ..." (ll. 6–9)
b) Rabia nods. "Do you know what he said to me?" Diane shakes her head.
"Only that I was showing too much." ...
Rabia nods. "He did. He meant it too. He thinks I'm immodest."
10 Diane shakes her head.
"He's just getting that from his friends ..." (ll. 32–34)

24 **Gesamtpunktzahl Aufgaben 1 und 2**

Kontrollieren Sie Ihre Ergebnisse mithilfe der Lösungen (S. 125/126) und addieren Sie die erreichten Punkte.

Teilbereich A: ☐ 24 bis 19 Punkte: ☺ ☐ 18 bis 12 Punkte: 😐 ☐ 11 bis 0 Punkte: ☹

B Referate

3 Körpersprache ist ein wichtiges Element in einer Präsentation. Worauf müssen Sie dabei besonders achten? Nennen Sie mindestens sechs Dinge.

Gesamtpunktzahl Aufgabe 3 6

C Lesen

4 Reading Comprehension: Tick the correct answers. Only one is correct.

a) The thought of Tahir being a good Muslim scares Diane because ...
   A ☐ he doesn't spend any time with the family anymore.
   B ☐ he forces his father to go to the mosque.
   C ☐ he has become a proud, serious young man.
   D ☐ he may be disillusioned or get hurt.

b) Tahir feels protected by his Muslim identity because ...
   A ☐ he visited his father's family in Pakistan and felt drawn to them.
   B ☐ he realises that there are tensions in the community and therefore feels a need for security.
   C ☐ he feels a sense of belonging.
   D ☐ he enjoys fasting and going to the mosque.

c) Tahir thinks his sister is immodest for wearing a revealing top because ...
   A ☐ he doesn't want his friends to stare at her.
   B ☐ she is too young to wear such clothing.
   C ☐ he is too pompous.
   D ☐ his Muslim friends have encouraged him to believe that women should cover themselves up.

d) Tahir thought the girl in the bikini he saw last summer ...
   A ☐ was certainly very nice to look at.
   B ☐ looked like a stalk.
   C ☐ was lustful.
   D ☐ was indecently dressed.

e) Suhail, Tahir's father, ...
   A ☐ was born in Pakistan.
   B ☐ married a non-Muslim.
   C ☐ disobeyed his parents.
   D ☐ has taught his son about Islam.

5

Kontrollieren Sie Ihre Ergebnisse mithilfe der Lösungen (S. 126) und addieren Sie die erreichten Punkte.

Teilbereich B: ☐ 6 bis 5 Punkte: 🙂 ☐ 4 bis 3 Punkte: 😐 ☐ 2 bis 0 Punkte: 🙁

5 Vocabulary: Decide which definition is the same or similar in meaning to the following words and expressions from the text.
Tick the correct answer (A, B, C or D).

a) miserable
A □ very unhappy B □ wicked C □ bad-tempered D □ angry

b) single-minded
A □ unmarried B □ strong-willed C □ unkind D □ arrogant

c) is bound to
A □ is ready to B □ is likely to C □ will feel sorry to D □ is tied to

d) are pulling apart
A □ are drifting apart B □ are moving closer
C □ are leaving the area D □ are becoming unfriendly

e) embarrassment
A □ irritation B □ enemy
5 C □ stranger D □ unpleasant feeling of shame

★ **6 Characterisation: Compare and contrast Tahir and Rabia based on the information in the text. (Write about 150 words)**

- Look at each character separately and describe them.
- Consider their similarities if there are any.
- Consider their differences.
- Read between the lines to get to the hearts of both characters.
- 16 Draw conclusions (infer).

★ **7 Speaking: The text contains information on the religious obligations in this Muslim family. Answer the questions. Make notes if necessary.**

a) What do the children in the text have to do according to their religion?
b) Are obligations important in teenage life?
c) Which obligations do you take seriously?
8 d) What would you expect from your friends in difficult situations?

34 **Gesamtpunktzahl Aufgaben 4 bis 7**

Kontrollieren Sie Ihre Ergebnisse mithilfe der Lösungen (S. 126) und addieren Sie die erreichten Punkte.
Teilbereich C: □ 34 bis 27 Punkte: ☺ □ 26 bis 17 Punkte: 😐 □ 16 bis 0 Punkte: ☹

D Schreiben

8 **Summarize the extract from "Caught in the Crossfire" in your own words. (Write about 150 words)** 6

9 **Comment Writing (300-400 words): Tahir had said to his sister when wearing her new top that "she was showing too much". (l. 30)**
Although Muslims might have stricter views on clothes, Christians also sometimes dislike the way some young girls dress today. So should we have the right to wear whatever we want to or should we be careful not to offend other people's feelings? Discuss the statement: Everyone in our modern society has the right to wear what he/she wants. 12

★ **10** **Creative Writing**
Write Rabia's diary entry in which she refers to her brother's comment that "she was showing too much". (200–250 words) 8

Gesamtpunktzahl Aufgaben 8 bis 10 **26**

E Mediation/Sprachmittlung

11 **Summarize the extract from "Caught in the Crossfire" in German. (Write about 150 words).**

Gesamtpunktzahl Aufgabe 11 **10**

Kontrollieren Sie Ihre Ergebnisse mithilfe der Lösungen (S. 126/127) und addieren Sie die erreichten Punkte.

Teilbereich D:	☐ 26 bis 21 Punkte: ☺	☐ 20 bis 13 Punkte: 😐	☐ 12 bis 0 Punkte: ☹
Teilbereich E:	☐ 10 bis 8 Punkte: ☺	☐ 7 bis 5 Punkte: 😐	☐ 4 bis 0 Punkte: ☹

Lösungen

Zur Bewertung der Tests:

→ Falls nicht in der Lösung anders angegeben, vergeben Sie pro Teilaufgabe einen Punkt – bzw. ziehen Sie pro Fehler einen Punkt ab. Sind Beispiellösungen angegeben, so bewerten Sie sich selbstkritisch.

→ Seien Sie vor allem beim Einstiegstest kritisch in der Bewertung: Er soll schließlich Aufschluss darüber geben, wo sinnvollerweise bevorzugt geübt werden soll.

Einstiegstest, Seite 7 bis 11

1
1. Who are the kids who have been bullying you?
2. How long have you been bullied?
3. Why have you never talked to us about it?
4. Haven't you got any friends who could help you at school?
5. Have you got any idea what caused these kids to do this to you?
6. What can we do for you now?

2 Mr Warren answered that he could give him a detention and said that what Steven had done had been wrong. He asked Jodee if she didn't think it would be better if she and Steve worked out their problem between the two of them without school intervention. He added that if he gave him a detention, she was only going to be labelled a tattletale. In the real world, they had to learn to fight their own battles.

3
3–5 My hands and feet were grabbed and I was dragged across the parking lot behind the main campus.
4 I was being kicked.
5 My bookbag was ripped open and the contents were thrown all over the ground.
28–29 ... so every afternoon when I got back from school, any evidence of abuse was carefully hidden.
32–33 When I was asked how school was going, I that everything was terrific and that I'd never been happier.

4 Possible answer:
You could read out the first 10–14 lines of Jodee Blanco's memoir to the class. It is always more gripping to start with a story or anecdote than just presenting the title of the presentation. The next step could be to include the class by asking about the reasons for the attack.

5 z. B.: Schriftgröße mindestens 20 pt, Farb- und Kontrastauswahl, jeder neue Aspekt auf eine neue Seite, nicht zu viel Schrift, keine zu unterschiedlichen Schriftarten, begrenzte Auswahl an Animationen, keine Orthographie- oder Tippfehler, etc.

6
a) ... dragged me across the parking lot behind the main campus. (l. 3–4)
b) Please, I can't be a tattletale again. I dreaded my parents finding out that I was a social failure again. (l. 19, 28)
c) Every eye in the room was on me. If I said anything to Ms. George, I'd be digging my own grave. (l. 24–25)
d) But don't you think it would be better if you and Steve worked out your problem between the two of you without school intervention? ... In the real world, we must learn to fight our own battles ... (l. 46 ff.)

7
a) A boy gripped her wrist and started twisting it until her knees began to buckle. Other students came at her from behind. They grabbed her hands and feet and dragged her across the parking lot behind the campus, chanting "We are going to kill you." They kicked her and spat on her. They threw her things around.
b) She carefully hid any evidence of abuse. She applied make-up over her whole body. She soaked her clothes. If she had to cry, she turned the stereo on.
c) She dreaded her parents finding out she was a social failure again.

8 Possible answer:
After Mr Warren's reply she felt very lonely. She asked herself why he did not really help her. Why do only tormentors have rights? What about the victims? I cannot understand

why he did not give him a detention. He had seen the incident. I could understand his reaction if he had only heard about the attack, but he observed us. Does he fear the parents? They are important people. Has he got problems with the same students in his lessons? Last week they behaved very aggressively towards him. But they do it in such an intelligent and subtle way that there is no possibility of punishing them for their behaviour. But he is an adult. He is my teacher. I expect more support. I need help. Should I ask him for help again? I cannot believe it. I feel so alone and frustrated. What will happen next time? Will my teachers only react after those bullies kill me?

9 Possible answer:
The extract from "Please stop laughing at me" is about the schoolgirl Jodee who has been bullied by some other kids. After the first of the two scenes of violence described in this extract she needs to go to a nurse who seems to know her and wants to contact her parents but Jodee refuses because she is afraid of the consequences (probably revenge) of telling the truth again. After the next attack on her she finally tells Mr Warren, a teacher who must know that something is wrong. She tells him that Steve, one of the bullies, hit her and wants the teacher to give him a detention. When Mr Warren advises her to cope with this on her own, she feels even more miserable than ever before.
(129 words)

10 Possible answer:
Being a student can be really hard. Sometimes it is not only difficult to get along with your teachers but also with your classmates. It seems as if there are students who are liked or admired by nearly everyone and others who are ignored or disliked. If this is the case and that student is even bullied by his classmates, then I think it is his right to demand help from his teachers. So I think what the teacher says to Jodee is only partly right. Wherever people are together, conflicts can arise. We are all different, have our own ideas, attitudes, likes and dislikes. Especially for young people it is not always easy to accept people who are different. Some of us are not even willing to be tolerant. There are people who think they have the right to hurt other people, because they don't like them for reasons which are hard to understand. But I think that nobody and nothing gives us the right to beat or hurt other people.
Some kids have been bullying Jodee. Her teacher, Mr Warren, is said to have known about this and he saw her crying when lying on the ground after Steve's attack. Jodee finally asks him for help. She wants Steve to get a punishment for what he did to her. The teacher refuses by saying that in real life we must also solve our problems on our own. Generally speaking, he is right. We as teenagers must learn to solve problems without teachers' interference. But this girl asks for his help. In such a situation a teacher should ask for details in order to be able to understand the whole situation and the reasons that led to it. And if a person like Jodee is in such a difficult situation, the teacher must help. At least he could have said that he must think it over and would like to talk to her again, but not this way, leaving her alone with all these problems.
(336 words)

11 Possible answer:
It was only years later, after I had left school, that a cousin of mine who attended the same school but a different class, told me why they had started bullying me. He had been standing close to some of the kids when he heard that they were talking about me.
They were making fun of me and laughing and having a great time. When asked why they were doing all this to me, they said that it was my own fault because some weeks before in Math class Steve, who had been called by the teacher, hadn't been able to give the correct answer because he hadn't done his homework and had gotten a bad grade for this and then I had raised my hand, given the right answer and had gotten a good grade for this. That was something they would never forgive me for and take revenge on me. So they started treating me that way ...
(159 words)

12 The enemy at my school
Thousands of boys and girls are being bullied physically (e.g. beating), or mentally (e.g. via mobiles or the internet), in Germany every day. A study found out that bullying is a serious problem at schools. Almost half of the students admit to be picked on by their mates and 20 percent are beaten up. Sometimes students use their mobiles to film the so called "happy slapping" and distribute the videos on the internet or via mobile.

Sprachliche Mittel – 1, Seite 12 bis 26

1 (1) fills (2) is moving
(3) manipulates (4) creates
(5) appear (6) is singing
(7) calls (8) speak
(9) form (10) is gaining
(11) is (12) is currently sharing
(13) plays (14) attributes
(15) is (16) still go
(17) are (18) find
(19) love (20) don't know
(21) don't have (22) fall
(23) gives (24) think
(25) can't (26) hear

2 a) correct b) is reading
c) ride d) exercises
e) correct f) correct
g) is falling h) correct
i) don't tell j) correct
k) call, is doing l) correct

3 (1) took part in (2) was held
(3) was (4) has just admitted
(5) felt (6) considered
(7) overcame (8) have earned
(9) was confirmed (10) won
(11) has taught (12) has given
(13) has gained (14) began
(15) have improved (16) have strengthened
(17) has been (18) have visited
(19) have had (20) reported

4 a) („rot" ist unterringelt)
has revolutionized (time until now)
has been surfing ... and building (started in the past and is continuing),
has found (indefinite time in the past),
has gained (past action with results in the present),
has increased (+ since: past action with results in the present),
has developed (past action with results in the present, no definite past time indicated/still holds true)

b) (1) has been carrying out
(2) has been troubleshooting
(3) has also been building
(4) has not always complied
(5) has not been exploited
(6) has been rewarded
(7) has completed
(8) has been neglecting/has neglected
(9) has proven
(10) have been flathunting
(11) has been scanning

5 a) was playing ... sneezed
b) was travelling ... died
c) were studying ... went off
d) was delivering ... exploded
e) began ... were still sitting
f) was raising ... declared
g) was ... were always nagging
h) was moving ... could not get
i) was only making ... shouted
j) were lining up ... made

6 [...] The second appearance of the ghost was on Sunday night. Shortly after the family had gone to bed they heard a fearful crash in the hall. A suit of armour had fallen on the floor and in a chair sat the Canterville ghost and rubbed his knees, which seemed to hurt. When the twins started shooting peas at him with their pea-shooters, the ghost stood up with an angry growl and passed through them like a mist. He also blew out the candle, leaving them all in total darkness. On top of the stairs the ghost turned around and, in order to frighten the Otis boys, laughed his most horrible laugh. Just then, a door opened and Mrs Otis came out of her bedroom. "I am afraid you are not well," she said, "I have therefore brought you this bottle of medicine." The ghost looked at her furiously, and then he disappeared. When he reached his room, he was completely exhausted. This American family was extremely annoying. But what annoyed him most was, that he had not been able to wear the suit of armour. The weight of it had made him fall and hurt his knees. [...]

7 Q: When did you start writing your own songs?
A: I started writing my own songs when I was 8 years old.
Q: Have you ever visited Lebanon?
A: Yes, I have. Arabic sounds have influenced my music ever since.
Q: Is it true that the Columbian singer Juanes is a big fan of yours?
A: Yes, he is. He is a wonderful man who has always been very encouraging.
Q: I heard that you have taken a particular interest in politics.
A: Yes I have. As I was born in Colombia, politics have always been important to me. When you live there you are always involved in politics.
Q: Have you been able to keep your Latin American creativity with your new English language songs on the" Laundry Service Album"?
A: Well, writing in English has been a real challenge. I spent a lot of time beforehand reading English poetry and that certainly helped.
Q: Can we expect to hear more English songs from you?
A: Definitely. That doesn't mean I will not also continue to write songs in Spanish.
Q: I have one final question before time runs out. When are you going to launch your next album?
A: It will be much sooner than you think.
Q: Thank you for your time. We are looking forward to your new release.
A: You're welcome. It was nice talking to you.

8 (1) is going to be
(2) is going/goes
(3) is going to live/will be living
(4) will actually live/am actually going to live
(5) am going to see/will see
(6) will have
(7) are going to go
(8) will be/is going to be
(9) will be
(10) will be
(11) will speak
(12) is going to be/will be
(13) will talk
(14) will even be able to
(15) will do
(16) is going to feature/will feature
(17) is going to be
(18) will miss
(19) will be
(20) will have spoken
(21) am going to be surrounded/will have been surrounded/will be surrounded
(22) will have experienced
(23) will have learnt

9 a) She is going to live in Wollongong, New South Wales, Australia.
b) She will see kangaroos and koalas every day.
c) She will miss her family and friends.
d) She thinks having to speak English all the time will be difficult, but it is going to be/ will be the greatest experience she (has) ever had.
e) She will be taking calculus, English Literature, History and foreign languages.
f) Only one student, Allison, will be going / is going to Australia this year.

Zwischentest, Seite 25 bis 26

1 **sentence:** Music experts say there is a general revival of the guitar today.
tense: simple present
why: genereller Fakt, auf die Gegenwart bezogen (heute)
sentence: This is changing as more and more young women are playing the guitar.
tense: present progressive
why: eine gegenwärtige, vorübergehende Erscheinung; andauernder Prozess
sentence: ... but recently the music scene has seen the great success of "girl bands".
tense: simple present perfect
why: ein Ereignis, das erst kürzlich geschehen ist und noch Auswirkungen hat
sentence: Last year people in the UK spent £105 million on guitars.
tense: simple past
why: abgeschlossene Handlung in der Vergangenheit (letztes Jahr)

2 a) My friend says we are a musical(ly gifted) family.
b) My mum can sing really well and she plays the flute.
c) My dad started to play the violin when he was five, so he is very good at it.
d) I've been playing the guitar for two years.
e) At the moment I'm taking piano lessons.
f) Next month my six-year old sister is going to join a choir.

Sprachliche Mittel – 2, Seite 27 bis 48

1
a) My sister and I went to see the new Star Wars film, which was one of the best films she had seen this year.
b) Susan would really like to go to the Miley Cyrus concert which will be in Munich.
c) The school books which were scattered on the floor belonged to Milton/The school books scattered on the floor belonged to Milton
d) In-line skating, which helps to strengthen your muscles, is a great way to keep fit.
e) My mother, who also carries on long phone conversations with her friends, is always complaining about the amount of time I spend on the telephone.
f) Bullying, which we have been having class discussions on, is a serious problem in schools/We have been having class discussions on bullying, which is a serious problem in many schools.
g) Roald Dahl, whose books are appreciated by adults and children, wrote Charlie and the Chocolate Factory.
h) Paul Kramer, to whom Employment Services of Disneyland/Florida made a part time job offer, is one of the students in our class./Paul Cramer, who is one of the students in our class, received/got a part-time offer ...
i) The book I am reading is Harry Potter and the Half-Blood Prince./I am reading a book which is called Harry Potter and the Half-Blood Prince.
j) David Beckham has a cool hairstyle, which I like a lot.

2
a) The English course which/that John applied for .../The English course John applied for ...
b) The lady who came into the ...
c) correct
d) He told me a story which/that I had already heard.
e) correct or They were the last group which handed/to hand in.
f) who they sent a letter to lives in a very remote area.
g) correct
h) Sandra, whose sister has been ...
i) Pollution in urban areas, which has become ...
j) correct

3
a) This evening I can pick up the tickets I ordered yesterday.
b) I have just read a review of the film/ movie I told my friend about two days ago.
c) Lily James, who plays the main character in "Cinderella", was in Berlin last autumn.
d) She plays a gir, who is raised without her mother, whose life changes when she meets a good-looking stranger.
e) There are people who go to the cinema/ movies just to see their favourtite actors.
f) In many small towns there are no cinemas, which is a shame/a pity.

4
a) being
b) to wear, keep
c) to sign in, to pick up
d) encouraging, to order
e) checking
f) eat, Hurrying
g) criticizing, know
h) to verify, checking, make
i) Accepting, to put, divide
j) satisfying, coming back, to show

5 spending, to allow, to attend, to stop, being, Gyrating, distributing, enhance, not to be, taking, become, lead, to inform, to enforce, know, curtailing, curbing, to end

6
a) Grinning
b) frightened
c) Hiding
d) tearing
e) spoken, written
f) Struggling
g) screaming
h) stuck
i) waiting
j) Driven

7
a) I saw a little girl playing with her dog.
b) Having read his girlfriend's e-mail, Robert phoned to thank her for the good advice she had given him.
c) I heard my teacher talking about an idea for a new project.
d) Arriving home Sarah opened all the windows because of a terrible smell inside the rooms.
e) Asked to resign because of his affair with a prostitute, the politician refused.
f) Seeing the new CD of her favourite singer in the shop, Janet decided to buy it immediately.
g) Susan ran to the bus stop talking to her friend on the phone to tell her she would be late.
h) Being Australian Nicole Kidman is proud of her origin.
i) I read the book "Junk" written by Melvin Burgess.

8
a) During my holidays I got to know an interesting American boy currently living in Berlin.
b) I met him at a party given by his German host brother.
c) I had heard the two boys talking about Josh's exchange year in Germany.
d) He came/had come to Germany wanting to learn more German.
e) Arriving at Munich airport he had the feeling he would never understand the Germans.
f) He watched a group of Bavarians talking about something he couldn't understand.
g) Josh remained standing there for a while thinking of/ and thought of returning home immediately.
h) However he stayed in Germany, making many friends.
i) Despite having made lots of friends here, he is looking forward to going home.
j) Asked if they wanted to visit Josh in the US, his host family accepted without hesitation.

9
a) He said he was going to Dublin for the U2 Concert.
b) He remarked he was not just seeing the band, he was helping with the show.
c) He said he would be helping set up the stage and the light show.
d) He pointed out it was an amazing thing and he couldn't believe it was happening to him.
e) He said he had been following the band throughout Europe on their last tour.
f) He said that in just under two weeks, he had seen them 10 times in 10 different cities.
g) He remarked that at every concert he had managed to get front row tickets, although sometimes they had been really expensive.
h) He said that after the eighth show, Bono had told him that he had seen him too many times and that he should join the road crew for the tour.
i) He said he was still going to University next year, but now he was enjoying an experience of a lifetime.

10
a) He asked Bono when he had given his first concert.
b) He wanted to know how they had become successful in Ireland.
c) He asked him if he had ever thought of becoming famous before their success.
d) He also wanted to know if he had enough time for friends despite his job.
e) Then he asked him what his plans for the next/for the following years were.
f) He asked him if he thought that he would still be on stage in 10 years.
g) He asked him if he could imagine doing another job.
h) Finally he wanted to know if he had ever been disappointed after a concert.

11
a) His mother asked him not to buy a new CD every week.
b) She asked him to tell her when he intended to go to a concert.
c) She warned him not to spend the night with people he didn't know.
d) She advised him to take a taxi home if the concert ended very late.
e) She asked him to bring her an autograph of her favourite singer.

12
a) The school is to be entered by the south doors only. All the other doors are locked until classes are over.
b) Running in the halls is not allowed.
c) A set of keys for all classrooms is kept by the school secretary.
d) Classrooms must be locked by students in charge of extra-curricular activities before they leave the building.
e) School property is not to be damaged.
f) Non-marking running shoes must be worn in the gym.
g) Lockers must be used for personal belongings.
h) You are expected to be on time for your classes. Latecomers must sign in at the principal's office.
i) If you are late three times, a letter is sent home to your parents.
j) Any student caught cheating in an exam will be suspended.
k) If a student has been given a red notice he (or she) must have it signed by his/her parents.

13
a) I'm sure you'll be asked ...
b) Questions on ... can be expected.
c) That's right, she's being interviewed.
d) Oh yes, ... has been conducted ...
e) ... applicants were really put through the wringer.

f) ... while he was being interviewed ... /... employees in personnel are being put, are put under pressure/... documents are not double-checked ... /... requirements have to be fulfilled ...
g) ... to tell you what needs to be worked on.

14 a) did b) will drive
c) went d) go on
e) hadn't learned/hadn't learnt

15 a) If John doesn't play football this season, the school team (will lose/would lose/would have lost) the championship.
b) More members would show up at our photography club meetings if we (make/would make/made) them more interesting.
c) I won't be angry if you (tell/told/will tell) the truth.
d) If drug dealers didn't exploit teenagers at clubs, they (might not/will not/wouldn't have) become addicts.
e) Writing letters the old-fashioned way may become obsolete if more people (would send/sent/sended) e-mails.
f) The orchestra wouldn't know how fast to play a piece if the conductor (didn't direct/wouldn't direct/hadn't directed) them properly.
g) Computer technology will expand even more if progress (continued/continues/will continue).
h) If you (have had/would have had/had had) more time, you could have helped me.
i) "Olivia and Raphael, you may not go swimming if you both (don't stop/won't stop/didn't stop) fighting right now!"
j) Do you think Sam (will go/would have gone/would go) to the dance with me if I had asked him.

16 Possible answer:
Hi Laura,
How's it going? I've intended to write to you since I got back from Paris, which, by the way, was a complete disaster. Jane, the friend I went with, was so bossy. If she had been more relaxed, we could have had a great time. I wish she hadn't chosen the hotel we stayed at. It was so expensive and if she hadn't, I might have had more money to spend. The other awful thing was that if she hadn't planned our daily itineraries, I might have been able to see some of the things I wanted to. Had Janet not been so afraid of taking the metro, we could really have explored the city. I would have wandered around and probably discovered some of the less touristic places if Janet hadn't insisted on taking the bus everywhere. Like you always say, I really need to be more assertive. If only I hadn't tried so hard to please her. Oh well.
You know how I love couscous and other kinds of food. Well, if Janet had been more adventurous about trying new dishes or having meals in places other than French cafes, I could have eaten some pretty authentic North African and Vietnamese food. And it would have been such fun to buy meals at the outdoor markets – even just a hunk of cheese and a baguette and eat it in the parks. Wait till you hear this one. I could have gone to the flea market at Clignancourt if she hadn't thought it would be dangerous and we could get robbed! Janet went to bed at 9 o'clock every night so when I did go out, I went alone. If I hadn't made an effort to speak French, we wouldn't have had any contact with the locals. Janet refused to even give it a try although she's taken French at school for five years.
Well Laura, sorry I've dumped this on you, but you can imagine how frustrated I am. Maybe next year, I'll have more luck. Write to me soon
Love,
Miriam

Zwischentest, Seite 46 bis 48

1 **active:** Last year people in the UK spent £105 million on guitars.
passive: Ten years ago £30 million was spent on guitars in the UK.
Bildung: Form von be + past participle

2 a) Bob Dylan is regarded as one of the most important musicians of rock and pop music.
b) Famous songs like "Knockin' On Heaven's Door" and "Like A Rolling Stone" were written by Bob Dylan.
c) "Blowin' In The Wind" – one of his first hits – was written in the 1960s.
d) His first rock double album "Blonde On Blonde" was released in 1966.
e) Another popular song from the album Desire, "Hurricane", was recorded in 1975 and released one year later in 1976.

f) Other singers and musicians like REM, U2 and Sheryl Crow were/have been influenced by him.
g) At the beginning of the 21st century Bob Dylan was awarded the Oscar for his composition "Things Have Changed".
h) Surely, his songs will also be heard, played and sung in the future.

3 a) *past participle* anstelle eines Relativsatzes: Five years ago in the US, Tish Ciravolo, a bass guitar player, set up the first company to produce **guitars which are made for girls**.
b) *present participle* anstelle eines Relativsatzes: Tish says, "What I wanted to do was not only design a guitar for a girl to play, but to change the consciousness – make the sight of **a girl who is playing the guitar as natural as that of a girl who is playing the flute**.
c) *gerund* nach Präposition

4 a) Last week Britney bought a guitar offered for £160 in a music shop in London.
b) She had watched the shop assistant showing different flutes to a woman and her child.
c) Having bought the new instrument she wanted to try it out immediately. After buying ...
d) At the moment Britney is sitting in her bedroom playing her new guitar.

5 a) **A piano** is a large keyboard instrument that is played by depressing black and white keys that cause hammers to strike strings.
b) **A concert** is a musical event/performance which is attended by lots of people who come to listen to one or several musicians or singers.
c) **A song** is a text which can rhyme and is usually sung.
d) **A guitarist** is a person who plays the guitar.
e) **An orchestra** is a large group of musicians playing different kinds of instruments.
f) **A CD** is a small plastic disc on which data like music can be stored. You can put it in a CD player to listen to it.

6 Conditional Typ I

7 1. C (III) 2. D (III) 3. E (I) 4. A (II) 5. B (I)

Sprachliche Mittel – 3, Seite 49 bis 61

1 a) Ben never goes to the supermarket in the evening.
b) Kevin often spends his afternoons in the park reading a book.
c) Jenny has been living in this wonderful town for more than 12 years now.
d) After Alan had seen the new film, he went to bed.
e) Although Frank was terribly ill, he came to the meeting.
f) I phoned my friend because I wanted to know where the concert was held.
g) They went to the cinema in order to see the new Tarantino film.
h) While my parents were taking a walk with our dog, I was surfing the net.
i) Have you ever seen such a fascinating show?
j) Where did you buy the jacket I like so much?

2 a) Who did the Millers talk to?
b) Where did the Milllers stay?
c) When did the Millers arrive?
d) Where has Alec never been to?
e) How long are the Millers going to stay in Spain?
f) Why do Kate and Alec have to share a room?
g) Who spent 50 € on her summer dress?
h) How did the Millers go to Spain?
i) What did Kate discover in her bed?
j) What sights in Barcelona did Mr and Mrs Miller visist?

3 a) Hardly had I come home when the storm started.
b) Not only are taxes annoying but also necessary.
c) Under no circumstances must the rules be broken.
d) Never had he thought that he would win the lottery.

4 1. Never have I been in such an excellent hotel before.
2. No sooner had we arrived at the hotel than the porter asked to take our luggage to our room.

3. However, not only did they look after us in a very welcoming way, but the hotel's restaurant was also delicious.
4. Only later did I find out that the hotel is highly recommended by several web pages.

5 Before you jump into this, Sue, I think:

a) You should/ought to find out if your shots are up to date, especially for tetanus and hepatitis. This can/could save you a lot of trouble later on.
b) You really must/have to shop around before you decide on a piercing shop. There are a lot of quacks out there.
c) The piercer you finally choose should/ must be qualified and experienced. You might/may want to have a look at his/her portfolio. And he absolutely has to/must wear gloves.
d) The shop itself has to/must be clean, safe and professional. There should be an autoclave for sterilizing equipment on hand.
e) The person performing the piercing has to/must thoroughly clean the area you're going to have pierced with a proper antiseptic soap. Otherwise the area might become infected.
f) The needle used must be sterilized and clean.
g) The stud must/has to be sterilized before he attaches it to your lip.
h) The pierced area has to/must be cleaned.
i) Remember, Sue, the piercer should give you specific instructions on how to look after your piercing.
j) You should know what steps need to be taken if the pierced area gets infected. I know this may sound too much but believe me, it's all for your own good.

6
a) Sarah will have to wear school uniform.
b) Sarah will not be able to phone her friends every day.
c) Sarah will not be allowed to go barefoot in the grass because of spiders and snakes.
d) Sarah will not have to get up so early in the morning because school starts at 9 o'clock.
e) Sarah will have to use sunscreen every day.
f) Sarah will be able to go surfing at the weekends.

7 Possible answers:

a) They had to work hard/help their parents every day.
b) At the weekend they were allowed to go to the cinema/walk in the park with their friends.
c) They weren't allowed to go to the disco every day.
d) They weren't able to play computer games or use mobile phones.

8
a) more modern
b) Better
c) (much) more
d) Less
e) worse
f) easier ... well/better
g) extremely ... highly
h) better ... more successful
i) slower
j) most important ... most needed

9
a) In high school overall grades are mostly based on continuous assessment.
b) Students generally receive ...
c) In order to graduate from high school, one has to have accumulated the required number of credits by the end of grade twelve.
d) Until now, university ...
e) Moreover, we do not have ...
f) High school students in Germany are seldom given a second chance ...
g) Unfortunately, Canadian tertiary institutions have higher tuition costs than German ones.
h) Students who have completed grade twelve successfully can enter community colleges.
i) School children at the age of 10 are often placed under enormous pressure in Germany.

10
a) Various PISA studies show that German students' results are often not as good as those of other European countries.
b) Unfortunately, not all students graduate successfully from secondary school.
c) You can often find more motivated students at more modern and better equipped schools.
d) Urgently needed/required reforms of the school system take quite long in Germany.

Zwischentest, Seite 61

1

positive	comparative	superlative
famous	more famous	most famous
light	lighter	lightest
narrow	narrower	narrowest
good	better	best

2 a) A local politician can be powerful. The German chancellor is more powerful than a local politician. The US President is the most powerful person of the three.
b) A record player is more modern than a gramophone, but the CD-player is the most modern way of listening to music.
c) An autograph can be interesting. An interview is usually more interesting. The most interesting thing is a live concert.
d) A crossword puzzle can be difficult. A test is more difficult. An exam is the most difficult thing of the three.

3 a) Second you **have to** practise.
b) If you **can't**, or don't have the money to pay for lessons, then you can use a book or just learn to play your favourite songs.
c) Third, you **should** find a band.

4

modal auxiliaries	substitutes
can	be able to
can, may	be allowed to
must	have to

5 a) couldn't/wasn't allowed to/wasn't able to
b) could/was able to
c) had to/was allowed to
d) cannot

Referate, Seite 62 bis 71

1 Ein möglicher Einstieg wäre z. B. eine Anekdote eines Australienreisenden, der über seine Erfahrungen mit der dortigen Tierwelt auf humorvolle Weise berichtet. Diese Geschichte können Sie vorlesen und zur Visualisierung Bilder der verschiedenen Tiere verwenden.
***Australia really is a dangerous place** to grow up. I remember staying at my friend's place for sleep over and every night we would have to patrol the floors in the deep shag pile carpet searching for and killing several of the deadly **Funnel Web Spiders** that had crawled inside each night, then we would check the walls for poisoness **Red Back Spiders**. I also remember fishing them out of another mates swimming pool. Every time we wanted to go for a swim we would have to **check the pool for spiders** first. We'd also have to check shoes before you put them on, and under the toilet seat before you sat down, in fact pretty much everywhere. And when you walked in the bush it was advised to step loudly giving the snakes ample warning so they could get out of your way – you did not want to come across an aggressive **Brown Snake, Red Bellied Black Snake**, just the **Common Death Adder**, or another other of our fabulous animal friends. Oh ... yeah and don't go swimming north of Brisbane. The beaches are beautiful but they are inhabited by Great **White Sharks, deadly Man-O-War Jellyfish, Salt Water Crocodiles**, the fresh water rivers have Crocodiles too and if you thought it was safe to hang around rock pools by the shore you will want to check out the cute but the (deadliest ocean dweller) **blue ringed octopus**.*
(aus: Douglas Adams, Life, The Universe, and Everything. © 1982, Pan Books)

2 Beispiellösung
Sie könnten die deutsche und die kanadische Flagge auf zwei Blätter malen. Für die kanadische Flagge benutzen Sie ein DIN-A3-Blatt und für die deutsche Flagge nehmen Sie ein Stück Papier etwa in der Größe einer Briefmarke. Jetzt falten Sie die kanadische Flagge auf die Größe der deutschen Flagge. Zu Beginn zeigen Sie nur die deutsche Flagge. Wenn Sie danach Kanada vorstellen, falten Sie die kanadische Flagge auf.
So bekommen Ihre Zuhörer eine bessere Vorstellung der Größenverhältnisse.
„*You all know this country.* (Zeigen der deutschen Flagge) *We live on 360.000 km²* (square kilometres). *Well, let's have a look at another country. This one has nearly 10 million km²!*" (Auffalten der kanadischen Flagge)

3 Hier würde sich anbieten einen Ausschnitt aus einem aktuellen Vampirfilm, wie z. B. „Twilight" oder der Serie „Vampire Diaries" zu zeigen. Alternativ könnten Sie auch eine passend ausgewählte Textstelle aus einem Vampirbuch vorlesen.

4 Rosa Parks Date of birth: February 4, 1913
Date of death: October 24, 2005
Most historians date the beginning of the modern civil rights movement in the United States to December 1, 1955. That was the day when an unknown seamstress in Montgomery, Alabama refused to give up her bus seat to a white passenger. This brave woman, Rosa Parks, was arrested and fined for violating a city ordinance, but her lonely act of defiance began a movement that ended legal segregation in America, and made her an inspiration to freedom-loving people everywhere.
Possible answer:
In December 1955, Rosa Parks, a 42-year-old black woman, didn't give up her bus seat to a white person. In Montgomery/Alabama, where the incident happened, and all over America this was not allowed and an offence against all white people. So/As a result, the police put her into prison. This act was the beginning of a very important movement in the United States which is called the Civil Rights Movement. It is so important because it ended legal segregation in America. (Hier solltest du den feststehenden Begriff ‚legal segregation' erklären)

5 Siehe unten

6 Die Checkliste sollten Sie vor Ihrer nächsten Präsentation in Englisch zusammenstellen und auf Ihr Thema anpassen. Lesen Sie dazu noch einmal die einzelnen Unterpunkte des Kapitels *Presentation/2-minute-speech* genau durch.

Zwischentest, Seite 71

1 Der Unterschied zwischen einer *2-minute-speech* und einer *presentation* liegt vor allem im Einsatz von Medien. Während bei einer *presentation* die Medien eine bedeutende Rolle spielen, sind sie aufgrund der zeitlichen Begrenztheit einer *2-minute-speech* kaum erforderlich.

2 a) Hier wird eine Idee vorgestellt, die das Publikum sofort zu Beginn aktiviert und seine Aufmerksamkeit sichert. Außerdem kann der Referent bereits einige sonst eher trockene Fakten im Quizformat nennen, die den Zuhörern auf diese Weise eher im Gedächtnis bleiben.
b) Diese Einführung weckt kaum das Interesse der Zuhörer. Sie ist monoton und sehr einfach aufgebaut. Der Referent hat sich keine besonderen Gedanken gemacht, wie er sein Publikum zum Zuhören motivieren kann.

Statue of Liberty

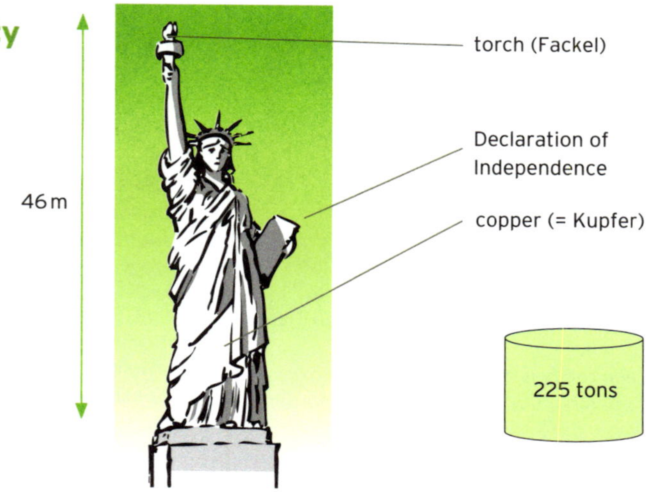

3 Anekdote, Fotos/Bilder, Quiz, Cartoon, Zitate, Hörbeispiele/Musik, überraschende Untersuchungsergebnisse, Witze, Auszug aus einer Geschichte, etc.

4 Medienverfügbarkeit, Funktionsfähigkeit der eingesetzten Medien, Aufbau vor der Präsentation, Kopien im voraus in guter Qualität erstellen (z.B. Farbkopien), Fernbedienung für Computerpräsentation organisieren, Plan B, etc.

Lesen, Seite 72 bis 84

1

adequate	apt	(l. 18)
apart from that	beyond that	(l. 21)
chased	haunted	(l. 3)
enormous	vast	(l. 20)
murder	homicide	(l. 15)
without any doubt	indisputably	(l. 4)

2 Possible Answer

Michael Jackson

✝ June 25th, 2009, memorial service in L.A.
Age: 50 years old
Albums sold: 750 millions
Target: because of surreal personal life, shocking scandals, serial plastic surgeries and eccentric public behavior
Jackson's death: died of pills and drugs; doctor of Jackson in the centre of investigation
Got famous as: a singer, songwriter, dancer and celebrity icon
Popularity compared to: Elvis Presley, the Beatles and Frank Sinatra

3 Possible answer:
Michael Jackson is such an ambivalent character for different reasons.
On the one hand he was a very famous and successful celebrity, who was talented in different fields such as singing, dancing and song writing. Jackson also made it into the Hall of Fame and earned countless awards. His huge influence on people is undeniable.
His extravagant behaviour however often caused shocking scandals and disapproval among the public. Plastic surgeries, drug and medicine abuse, as well as/in addition to life-style turned him into a tragic figure in the entertaining world.

4
a) General information about Sydney, sights, recreational areas/leisure, accommodation, food and entertainment
b) Sydney Opera House, Darling Harbour, Art Gallery of New South Wales, Sydney Tower, Harbour Bridge, Mrs Macquarie's Point
c) hotels, hostels, bed & breakfast, camping facilities

5
a) It is the harbour with the Opera House.
b) It is compared to Manhatten/New York City.
c) The highest structure is the Sydney Tower.
d) I would go to Kable's or Doyle's.

6
a) ... there are people from many different ethnic backgrounds living there.
b) ... protect swimmers from shark attacks/ to prevent sharks from entering the swimming areas.
c) ... you can always buy restricted view tickets or try getting last minute, half-price ones at Halftix.
d) ... should visit the Art Gallery in Sydney.
e) ... be seen at Balls Head Reserve.

7
a) Life is a brief candle, a walking shadow, a poor player, a tale told by an idiot, nothing.
b) The 'she' refers to Macbeth's wife.
c) 'All our yesterdays' is a metaphor for our past.
d) Macbeth's words evoke a melancholy/ tragic/sad mood. The character feels broken and remorseful.
e) 'Sound and fury' remind us of those moments in our life which are turbulent and challenging causing anger and desperation.
f) 'Dusty' is used to signify what remains of us after death – only ashes, dust. For Macbeth, there is no notion of life after death.

8

Noun	Adjective
fury	**furious**
significance	**significant**
record/recording	recorded
pettiness	petty
fool	**foolish**

10
- "An extraordinary achievement" (Sunday Times)
- "A terrifically entertaining and imaginative story wrapped round its tough, thought-provoking philosophical heart" (Independent on Sunday)
- "Sophie's World is set to become a unique popular classic: a wonderfully engaging mystery story that also forms a completely accessible and lucid introduction to philosophy and philosophers" (The Times)

11
- collecting old coins or foreign stamps
- doing needle work
- spending time on a particular sport
- enjoying reading/reading tastes differ, newspaper, comics, novels, books on astronomy, wildlife, technological discoveries
- being interested in horses or stones
- watch all the sports programs on TV

12 Basic needs: food; warmth, love, care; company of others
Philosophical interests/questions:
- What is the most important thing in life?
- Why are we here?
- Who are we?

But when these basic needs have been satisfied – will there still be something that everybody needs?

13 An excerpt from a novel, a letter to Sophie the main character

14 The debate is as old as the mankind itself.

Zwischentest, Seite 84

1

a) F	b) F	c) F	d) NI
e) F	f) T	g) T	h) F
i) T	j) NI	k) F	l) T

2 ... Peacock added sentimental ...
Despite their initial arguments ...
But it also means that the viewer of ...
If you can peel away ...
But you have to work at it.

3

a) assumes	b) pride
c) argue	d) tense
e) shame – guilt	

Schreiben, Seite 85 bis 99

1 Mögliche Faktensammlung zur Beantwortung der fünf Fragen:

Frage	Antwort
where	at an American high school
when	in our time, present
who	Three students: Karen & Julie, Miriam
what	bullying leading to suicide attempt
why	bullying for fun, Miriam not popular, writes poetry; tries to commit suicide after the girls have made her think that the whole class hate her

Possible answer: *Summary of "Locker 160"*
The story "Locker 160" is set at a school in the USA in our time.
Two girls named Karen and Julie bully their classmate Miriam just for fun.
Having chosen her for no special reason apart from her being different because she writes poetry and is not popular, Karen and Julie play different nasty tricks on her. The last one – a note saying that all her classmates think she is weird and hate her – causes Miriam to attempt suicide, but she is saved just in time.
When Karen and Julie get to know this, they show no sign of regret or pity.
(102 words)

2 Possible answer:
The story of "The Meeting" is set in Johannesburg, South Africa during the time of Apartheid. It is about two 17-year-old girls who happen to meet each other near a park one day. Candy, who is white, twists her ankle and is offered help by Becky, a pretty black girl. While talking they get to know each other a little, and Candy realizes that she likes her despite her initial mistrust caused by her upbringing. Before Candy phones her father to fetch her, the girls agree to meet again. When Candy's father arrives, he shows no interest in Becky although his daughter praises her so much. Finally he realizes that Candy wants him to thank her as well but, misunderstanding the whole situation, offers her a tip, which Becky refuses and considers an insult. (134 words)

3 Possible answer:
Becky suddenly turned and walked off.
Meanwhile Candy's father got impatient. "Why doesn't she want to take the money? Isn't

it enough?!" he asked his daughter. Instead of answering his question, Candy shouted, "Becky, please wait!" To her father's surprise, Becky was running away.
"Let's get into the car," he said. While driving home, Candy tried to explain to her father what had happened. But he didn't really understand. So Candy didn't tell him about their intention to meet again since she was afraid he wouldn't allow her to see Becky again anyway. In the evening, when Candy was lying in bed, she thought about what to tell Becky next Wednesday when they would meet again. She was wondering how she could explain her dad's behaviour to her and say sorry. Hopefully Becky would come as Candy wished so much. There were so many things she wanted to talk about with her ...
(152 words)

4 Possible answer:
Candy and her father drove off. On their way home Candy said nothing for a while.
Dad: Why are you so quiet? What's wrong with you? Does your foot still hurt?
Candy: No, it's not because of my foot. It's ... you know ... I mean ... How could you be so rude to Becky?
D: You call me rude? What are you talking about? She is just a black girl. Should I have invited her to dinner tonight?
C: Please, be serious.
D: I am serious. She helped you and that's nice, I understand, but don't you think she was rude when she refused the money I offered to her? Is she too proud to accept a tip from a white man? It's obvious she's poor. She was wearing such terrible, ragged clothes! By the way, have you still got your purse? I wouldn't be surprised to find out that she ran away with it!
C: But dad, that's exactly what I thought at the beginning, too. But you are being unfair. It's the same old story you've been telling me my whole life. Blacks are inferior, dirty, dishonest, uneducated ...
D: And it's true!
C: No dad, it isn't. Becky is wonderful. She is pretty and has a good sense of humour. She made me laugh several times although I was in pain. And of course she is honest. She didn't rob me. And by the way, do you know why she didn't take your money? She didn't want it because you don't pay a friend for helping you.
D: A friend?
C: Yes, we've become friends and I'm looking forward to seeing her again.
D: You won't see her again. A black and a white girl can't be friends, not in our society. Don't forget this! So, here we are at the doctor's. I want Mr Deep to check your foot. And please no talking about that black girl any longer.
Candy decided not to tell her dad about their agreement to meet each other again ...
(339 words)

5 Possible answer:
Throughout the history of mankind people have oppressed each other. The white man conquered the native people of America and Australia, as well as the blacks he had taken from Africa as slaves, to name just a couple of examples.
So, are some people more equal than others or are all people equal, no matter who they are or where they are from? In my opinion there can only be one answer to this question: As we are all human beings, it goes without saying that we are all equal. On the other hand, reality shows that racial prejudice still exists and inequality can be found all over the world.
Nearly 150 years ago, Abraham Lincoln put an end to slavery with the Emancipation Declaration of 1863, which was only put into practice after the end of the Civil War two years later. Then a time of segregation followed which lasted as long as the Civil Rights Movement when Martin Luther King fought for equal rights for black people. Finally, black people as well as Native Americans were granted full rights. But does this really mean that they were then or are really equal to whites today? According to the law, they are, but more subtle forms of racial discrimination have replaced the obvious ones. Of course, we all know famous and successful Afro-Americans – just think of actors, singers and sportsmen. But what about the high unemployment rate among blacks or the high proportion of black people on death row? Moreover, there are parallels to this development when we look at South Africa after the time of Apartheid or at what is happening to Aborigines in Australia.
In addition, globalisation causes the widening of the gap between rich and poor. Still and,

perhaps, more than ever the developed countries benefit from the so called developing countries, thus leading to more political, economic and social inequalities. With the attack on September 11, 2001 and Bush's war on terrorism, tensions between Muslims and the western world have grown making it difficult to establish equality or simply a better understanding and tolerance of people of different origins and religious backgrounds.
All in all, there is no denying that we are all (biologically speaking) equal and no people have the right to say they are superior to other nations. But there are so many examples in history and at present which show that a lot of people, including leading politicians, do not accept this notion. This leads me to the conclusion that these inequalities will continue to exist in the near future. (428 words)

6 a) The action takes place at the counter of a public bar/café.
b) People and objects: a middle-aged man reading a newspaper; a teenager using an electronic tool to be up-to-date
c) Newspaper: symbol for the old-fashioned printing press;
Electronic tool: symbol for the bunch of information you can have access to anywhere in the world. Also symbol for new technology age.
d) A man and a boy are having a conversation at the counter of a public bar. The boy wants to know why the man still uses old-fashioned media instead of getting information from new internet applications like web-services, online communities or online shopping centres. The man responds by asking him for the sports section.

7 a) The speech balloons explain the possible applications of different kinds of media. The boy gives examples of new online services like Flickr, Google or Twitter, the man points out advantages of newspapers.
b) The people represent two generations. The man grew up with print media, whereas the boy belongs to a generation which is used to new technology and world-wide connections.
c) The cartoon may want to convey that each kind of media has its advantages and disadvantages. The boy uses new technology because he can get a load of information in a short time at any place in the world. The comment of the man criticizes the lack of structure and clarity and the time-consuming search for pieces of information.
d) New media is about to replace print media because of its numerous possibilities and its easy access to all kind of information. However, it brings a flood of information nobody can fully understand anymore. As newspapers lose many subscribers to the new media, it's necessary for them to find alternative ways of attracting especially the young generation.

Zwischentest, Seite 99

1 The cartoon satirizes modern communication and its excesses amongst youngsters using the example of social networks on the internet. It shows a teenage girl having a conversation with her parents at dinner. The father wants his daughter to tell him about her day but the girl seems to be indifferent and from her facial expression it would seem she doesn't see any sense in communicating about something her parents can read in her tweets.
The cartoon alludes to a current problem of modern society: people often spend too much time in social networks on the internet and start losing the ability and the interest to communicate face to face with others. Blogs, Twitter, Facebook etc. replace the necessity to meet friends and encourage unrealistic interpersonal communications. They give innumerous people access to your life which is, especially for the younger generation, much more important and maybe more comfortable than having a serious conversation.

Mediation/Sprachmittlung, Seite 100 bis 104

1 Well, the German teacher Richard Schirrmann, who lived between 1874 and 1961 came up with the idea of cheap accomodations for young people when he and his pupils were on

a hiking trip and only found shelter from a thunderstorm at a village school.
If you want to stay at any German youth hostel nowadays you need to be a member with the association DJH. You have to pay an annual fee and get a membership card.
There are quite some differences between hotels and youth hostels. One is that they have common rooms for young people to get to know each other and plan activities together. Not only will you get to know young people from all over the world at a youth hostel but you also learn a lot about Germany.

2 Eisenach:
Eisenach is a city in the state of Thüringen and it's well-known because of two celebrities. The first is Johann Sebastian Bach, one of the most famous German composers of classical music. You can visit the museum "Bachhaus" in Eisenach where you can learn about his work and life. The other celebrity is Martin Luther, who translated the bible into the German language. He hid in a castle called "Wartburg", which is close to Eisenach. There you can see the room where he worked.

Cuxhaven:
Cuxhaven is a town on the North coast of Germany. A popular free-time activity is to wander along the beaches, especially in spring time. When the tide is low you can walk on the soft, wet sandy ground, the "Watt". On organized theme walks you can learn something about the animals of the "Watt" or about the "Bernstein", a special yellow or brown stone used for making necklaces.

Zwischentest, Seiten 103 bis 104

1 Possible answer:
Kati Wilhelm: fourth gold medal in Vancouver 2010?
The German biathlete Kati Wilhelm has already won three Olympic Gold medals and is now preparing for the Olympic Games in Vancouver 2010. A couple weeks ago she visited my school and it was a fantastic experience for us because she answered all the questions we had.
As well as biathlon, obviously her favorite sports, she's especially interested in athletics and swimming in the summer and in cross-country skiing and ski-jumping in the winter.
When we asked her about doping she said that she was absolutely against it and in favor of strict controls.
It was very interesting to hear how much she earned. She explained that there are certain awards in different competitions for the top positions. In the world cup. for example, you can earn 10.000 Euros (before taxes) for the first place. Depending on how successful you are you can earn more money by being sponsored.
But money is not everything. The Olympic Games are a very special event for Kati Wilhelm because they only take place once every four years and that's why she is pretty nervous about participating in Vancouver. It's important for her to not be indifferent about everything.
Her family and friends are a central part in her life. They help her to deal with her success in an easy-going way. She's proud of her achievements but she tries to stick to her roots. Except for her team mates she doesn't have any famous friends but she sometimes meets celebrities like the Klitschkos, two famous German boxers.
We finally asked her if she smoked. She answered that smoking was very unhealthy and all her training would be worthless if she ruined her lung capacity.
Hopefully the Olympic Games in Vancouver will be successful for her again and we keep our fingers crossed for her. GO, Kati, GO!

Abschlusstest, Seite 105 bis 109

1
a) present progressive:
Verlauf einer Handlung in der Gegenwart, die noch nicht abgeschlossen ist.
b) past progressive: Verlauf einer Handlung in der Vergangenheit, noch nicht abgeschlossen zu dem Zeitpunkt als sie lächelte und gefragt wurde.
c) simple past:
Abgeschlossene Handlung in der Vergangenheit.
d) simple present:
Gegenwart, genereller Fakt, sich wiederholend.
e) simple present perfect:
Prozess, der in der Vergangenheit begonnen hat und bis zur Gegenwart anhält

f) present progressive + present perfect progressive: Gegenwart, jetzt gerade + Handlung , die in der Vergangenheit begonnen hat und bis zur Gegenwart anhält (je 2 P. für a bis e; 4 P. für f)

2 a) Diane explained that she had just been thinking about Tahir. She asked if Rabi remembered what he had been like when he had first started fasting.
Rabi laughed and answered that he had been so miserable.
Diane answered that she knew and that he hadn't been a very good Muslim at that time. (4 P.)

b) Rabia nodded and asked her mum if she knew what he had said to her. Diane shook her head. So Rabia added that she had been showing too much. She continued that he had said that and that he had meant it too. He thought she was immodest. Diane shook her head and finally said that he was just getting that from his friends. (6 P.)

3
- fester Stand
- Augenkontakt mit dem Publikum und nicht mit dem Lehrer
- Hände nicht in den Hosentaschen oder verschränkt vor der Brust
- nicht nervös herumlaufen
- sich nicht hinter einer Tafel oder einem Tisch „verstecken"
- keine hektische, dennoch lebendige Gestik
- kein „Herumfingern" mit Karteikarten oder Notizen
- aufrechte Körperhaltung, etc.

4 a) C b) B c) D d) A e) B

5 a) A b) B c) B d) A e) D

6
- Rahia and Tahir are siblings – similar upbringing and education – Rahia appears to be younger, but only slightly. Both are teenagers.
- Tahir has undergone a personality change due to rising tensions in the community where they live – latched on to Pakistani heritage for security – probably had to make a choice because the community is breaking up racially – Rahia is lighthearted (examples), close to mother – smiles when she smiles, they weep together whereas Tahir is now serious and pompous – Tahir is presumably no longer close to mother, sees her as an "embarrassment" – prompts father to go to mosque – reprimands his sister for wearing revealing clothing – determined to follow the rituals of muslim faith – gives him a feeling of identity – probably feels torn between his Englishness and his Pakistani ancestry. Maybe there is also a visible difference (skin colour, eyes, hair etc.)
- Rahia seems less concerned about these issues – close connection to mother suggests she feels strongly English, less torn.

7 a) To go to the mosque; to fast for Ramadan; to show great pride in their Pakistani ancestry; to care for family members, especially sisters

b) (Individual answers). Yes, of course, everyone needs obligations, especially young people. Young people must learn to take obligations seriously, they must feel responsible for others. (family members, friends, pets ...)

c) School, sport, friends, my job after school, helping my family members ...

d) They should grow into proud and open-minded individuals. They should trust their family and friends. They should learn at a very young age that they are responsible for themselves. (je 2 P.)

8 Possible answer:
The extract from "Caught in the Crossfire" is a talk between Diane and her daughter Rabia. They speak about Tahir, Rabia's brother, and how his character and attitudes have changed over time.
Although he wasn't a good Muslim when he first started fasting, he shows a lot of self-control today. Moreover, he now encourages his father to go to the mosque and seems to have become a serious young Muslim.
He is fully aware and proud of his Pakistani ancestry.
Diane and Rabia also talk about a disapproving comment Tahir made about a top Rabia had worn for a birthday party.
Although he considered his sister immodest, last summer he couldn't resist staring at some girls who had been wearing even less than his sister.
Whereas mother and daughter get along with each other really well, the mother seems to be

quite concerned about the changes in her son. (149 words)

9 Possible answer:
Ask young girls what they are interested in and most of them will answer: fashion. Not only girls, also boys and not only teenagers, but also adults pay a lot of attention to what they wear. Should we have the right to wear whatever we want to or consider what other people might think about it?
Generally speaking I think people in westernized countries wear whatever they want and I don't want to change this. On the other hand, there are situations when it's wise to make some compromises and think about the effect the choice of your wardrobe might have on other people.
Fashion is not only a matter of taste it also changes constantly. Look at photos of your parents when they were in their teens and you are likely to smile when you see what they wore at that time. Nevertheless, some trends appear again and again.
But a point that definitely concerns a lot of people nowadays is "how much we show" when wearing tops or miniskirts which show more than they conceal/cover. Although I like wearing such clothes a lot, there are occasions when I think that this way of dressing is unsuitable, for example when going to church, applying for a job or even for my very conservative grandma's birthday party. I like her a lot and don't want to upset her. I also have to accept a special dress code when I'm on holiday abroad and want to enter a church or a temple. I believe it's necessary to respect other people's religious beliefs and attitudes.
However, in my spare time and for school I want to wear what I like and I would surely disapprove of being forced to wear school uniform, as pupils in lots of other countries have to do.
Having considered all these issues I can only conclude that we should really have the right to wear what we want but at the same time be willing to accept that there are a few exceptions when we shouldn't offend other people's feelings. (343 words)

10 Possible answer:
Dear Diary,
Today we went to Sofia's birthday party and had a really great time. It was good to see lots of my cousins, aunts and uncles there. I always like being with my family. Sofia was happy about the nice presents she got. I gave her a beautiful scarf and I'm sure she likes it. The only thing that upset me was my brother's comment about my wonderful new top when he picked me up and took me home. Fortunately, he didn't say it in front of all the others, that would have been too embarrassing. Nevertheless I think his views are sometimes too strict. He said I was showing too much. First I thought he was kidding but a look at his face and also his voice told me he wasn't. He really meant what he said. But we don't live in Pakistan. We live here in Britain and now so I don't want to dress like my Pakistani aunts and grandmas – I am a British teenage girl! Doesn't he understand? Sometimes I think he really doesn't as he's so focused on his Muslim identity and all that stuff. But I'm not like him, I have other friends and other interests – that's something he has to accept.
Yours, Rabia (211 words)

11 Possible answer:
Der Textauszug aus „Caught in the Crossfire" beschreibt ein Gespräch zwischen Diane und ihrer Tochter Rabia. Sie reden über Rabias Bruder Tahir und wie sich sein Charakter und seine Einstellung mit der Zeit verändert haben.
Bevor er anfing, den Ramadan einzuhalten, war er kein streng gläubiger Muslim. Heute allerdings bringt er ein hohes Maß an Disziplin in Glaubensfragen auf und überzeugt sogar seinen Vater, regelmäßig in die Moschee zu gehen. Er ist sich seiner pakistanischen Wurzeln bewusst und sehr stolz auf sie. In ihrem Gespräch kommen sie auch auf einen abschätzigen Kommentar, den Tahir seiner Schwester gegenüber machte, als diese ein in seinen Augen zu freizügiges Oberteil trug. Obwohl er dies als unanständig erachtete, konnte er im letzten Sommer selbst nicht widerstehen, einigen Mädchen hinterher zu starren, die ähnlich freizügig gekleidet waren wie seine Schwester.
Der Auszug macht deutlich, dass sich Mutter und Tochter sehr gut verstehen, während die Mutter über die Entwicklung ihres Sohnes äußerst besorgt ist.

fit fürs
abi

Die Erfolgsreihe „Fit fürs Abi“

Fit fürs Abi Oberstufenwissen
Das komplette Oberstufenwissen, ausführlich und anschaulich erklärt. Mit Gratis-App: Wichtige Fachbegriffe nachschlagen!

Fit fürs Abi Klausur-Training
Beispiel-Klausuren mit Lösungen zu den wichtigsten Prüfungsthemen

Fit fürs Abi Express
Die wichtigsten Abiturthemen knapp und übersichtlich für den Endspurt. Mit Gratis-App: Express-Training fürs Abi!

ideal auch als Lernskript zu
„Fit fürs Abi Oberstufenwissen“

So punktest du im Abitur:
www.westermann.de/fit-fuers-abi

westermann